*How to Know*
# THE BIRDS

# *How to Know*
# THE BIRDS

### An Introduction to Bird Recognition
by
**ROGER TORY PETERSON**

With 72 full-color
illustrations by the author and
more than 400 line drawings

*Endorsed by*
*The National Audubon Society*

GRAMERCY PUBLISHING COMPANY
*New York*

# To My Mother

This 1986 edition is published by Gramercy Publishing Company, distributed by Crown Publishers, Inc., by arrangement with Houghton Mifflin Company.

The color illustrations in this book are taken from the gallery of the famous Wildlife Conservation Stamp Series. The National Wildlife Federation is a non-profit, non-governmental organization concerned with educating the people to the vital necessity of good management of our woods, soil and wildlife. For information on how you can help in this great work, write to National Wildlife Federation, 1412 16th Street, N.W., Washington, D.C. 20036

Printed and Bound in the United States of America

Library of Congress Cataloging-in-Publication Data

Peterson, Roger Tory, 1908-
  How to know the birds.

  Reprint. Originally published: 2nd ed. newly enl.
Boston: Houghton Mifflin, 1962, c1957.
  "Endorsed by the National Audubon Society."
  Includes index.
  1. Birds—United States—Identification.   I. Title.
QL682.P475   1985        598.2973        85-22004

ISBN: 0-517-49202-4

h g f e d c b a

# CONTENTS

*NOTE: Families are here arranged in the accepted systematic order but in the book a few departures have been dictated by convenience in presentation.

# PREFACE

Birds can fly where they want to when they want to. So it seems to us, who are earthbound. They symbolize a degree of freedom that we would nearly give our souls to have. Perhaps this is why bird watching has almost become a national hobby in Britain and is rapidly becoming one here. It is an antidote for the disillusionment of today's world, a world beset by pressures it has never before known. Many men in business and the professions find in birds a much-needed balance, a retreat from their highly complex affairs and the artificiality of the city. Housewives find in them a pleasant relief from the routine of the home, and children enjoy their pursuit for the release it gives their abundant energies. Boys in their teens make the keenest bird recorders, for once they fall under the spell of the "lure of the list," they play the game for all it is worth.

This small book was written mostly for those who have never had a bird guide before, but who are becoming aware of the multitude of birds with which we live. In it I have pointed out the short cuts to recognition. By applying its principles you can in one year gain a background that took most of us old timers several years to acquire. It is not even necessary to use field glasses if you know the silhouettes and field-marks of birds, but it must be admitted that a pair of eight-power binoculars makes each bird look eight times as handsome.

The thousands who already own my FIELD GUIDE TO THE BIRDS and the FIELD GUIDE TO WESTERN BIRDS, and who carry them in their pockets will, I believe, find this book useful as a sort of refresher course, even though the FIELD GUIDES are more complete in matters of field-marks, song, and range.

ROGER TORY PETERSON

7

# I.

# INTRODUCING THE BIRDS

## THIS IS AN EAGLE

The "King of Birds" is known to everyone. It is our national emblem.

When someone apologetically says that the only birds he knows are "a Robin and a Sparrow" he is under-estimating himself. He almost certainly can recognize a Crow, a Hummingbird, an Owl, a Duck, or even a Peli-can. A little questioning will probably reveal that he knows three or four others. Most surely he can tell what an Eagle is, though very likely he has never seen a live one. If he were to dip into his pocket or billfold he would probably find half of the coins or bills in his possession emblazoned with its heroic figure.

It is impossible not to know an Eagle.

1. Monkey Eating Eagle (Philippines) ; 2. Harpy Eagle
(South America); 3. Bateleur Eagle (Africa); 4. Steller's
Sea Eagle (Siberia) ; 5. Crested Eagle (Burma).

# BUT THERE ARE MANY KINDS OF EAGLES

At least *fifty* species of big birds of prey are called "Eagles." They range over every continent in the world.

The term "Eagle" is a loose one, hard to define. Some of our "Buzzard Hawks," like the Red-tailed, Red-shouldered, and Broad-winged Hawks, belong to the same sub-family (*Buteoninae*). Perhaps the best definition of the term is that it is generally given to the larger Hawks, particularly those with longish heads and big bills.

Although some of the big fellows like the Harpy of Central America and the Monkey-eating Eagle of the Philippines (see opposite) are powerful enough to carry off a baby, they never do. Such goings on are pure fiction, which is the way some irresponsible newspaper editors like their natural history. Certain Eagles can fly fast enough to strike down birds in flight. Others capture fleet-footed rabbits. But others, less energetic, specialize in snakes or fish. Our Bald Eagle just can't resist robbing the Osprey of its catch when it can intercept the hard-working "Fish Hawk" on its way home. Usually, however, it searches the beaches for dead fish cast up by the waves. Some Eagles relish carrion and are almost Vulture-like in their habits.

So you can see that Eagles are a diverse lot. There are huge ones, capable of catching and lifting monkeys and wild pigs. Others are scarcely larger than Crows. Some are handsomely patterned with white wing patches; others have crests. Tails vary from wedge-shaped rudders to the ridiculously stubby one of the Bateleur of Africa (see opposite), a tail-less appearing Eagle that looks like a radical aviation experiment—sort of a flying wing.

Of all this virile tribe, America has only two, the Golden Eagle, a golden-naped bird of the mountains, and the Bald Eagle, our national emblem, identified by its white head and tail. Both should be protected at all times lest we lose them as certain European countries have lost their Eagles. Fortunately, in some states such as Florida, residents are very proud of their Eagles and cherish them.

11

1. Vulture; 2. Lady Amherst Pheasant; 3. Bell-Bird;
4. Penguin, 5. Marabou Stork; 6. Toucan; 7. Cassowary;
8. Macaw; 9. Kiwi.

# EAGLES REPRESENT ONLY ONE BIRD FAMILY

An Ostrich sometimes weighs more than 300 pounds. A Ruby-throated Hummingbird tips the scales at less than one-tenth of an ounce. An Ostrich, then, weighs nearly 50,000 times as much as a Ruby-throat. Still, the latter is not nearly so small as the Bee Hummingbird of Cuba, the world's tiniest feathered creature.

The diversity in the appearance of birds is as fantastic as their range in size. Compare a Penguin with its flightless seal-like flippers to the Wandering Albatross with its eleven-foot sails. Or contrast the homely, hairy-looking Kiwi (see opposite), devoid of wings, to a Peacock or a Bird of Paradise! Flamingoes have incredibly long necks and equally long legs, while Whip-poor-wills seem neckless and have such tiny legs that they might as well have none. Bills show every imaginable adaptation; there are the thick seed-cracking bills of Finches, pruning-shear bills of Crossbills, slender probing bills of Snipe and Hummingbirds, chisel bills of Woodpeckers, spear bills of Herons, saw-toothed bills of Mergansers, shovel bills of Ducks, hooked beaks of Hawks and Owls, and the huge colorful probosci of Toucans. Swimming like an unladen sloop, diving like a submarine, wading, running, climbing, soaring or plunging through the air like a spent rocket are only a few of the accomplishments of the feathered galaxy whose myriad members are decked in every color of the rainbow.

According to the careful estimate of Dr. Ernst Mayr of the American Museum of Natural History, there are about 8,600 species of birds in the world. Other scientific men have put the figure between 13,000 and 16,000. This disparity is because they differ with Mayr in their definition of a species and include many birds that Dr. Mayr would regard only as well-marked local races (subspecies) of other species. James Fisher, the British ornithologist, states that there are about 28,000 species and subspecies of birds in the world. But we won't concern ourselves with the whole world. In this book we will deal only with North America.

# NORTH AMERICA HAS 650 SPECIES OF BIRDS

Add to this about 100 accidentals—waifs from Europe that have crossed the Atlantic, storm-blown strays from the West Indies, Mexican birds that have wandered across the border, and Asiatic birds that have infiltrated to Alaskan outposts—and you have the number of species that have been recorded in North America north of the Mexican boundary.

But if *subspecies* are included, the number is closer to 1500. Lest you are puzzled let me explain. A subspecies is a geographic race that differs very slightly from other races of the same species. To illustrate; the Robins that live on the foggy island of Newfoundland differ from those of eastern Canada in being darker on the back, so they are called by a different name (Black-backed Robin). The others are called Eastern Robins. They are all Robins however, and if a Black-backed Robin for some reason failed to attempt the flight across the Gulf of St. Lawrence in spring, it could theoretically mate with an Eastern Robin, and raise a family, just as a fair-haired, blue-eyed Swede might marry a dark-haired, dark-eyed Italian. Species, on the other hand, are *reproductively* isolated. A Robin would not mate with a Wood Thrush, nor would a Song Sparrow pair with a Chipping Sparrow.

Museum men have "split up" the Song Sparrows of North America into twenty-seven different subspecies. Although the ones found in the desert are so small and pale as to be markedly different from the large dark birds of the Aleutians, most subspecies of the Song Sparrow are so much alike that to determine to which one a bird belonged, you would have to hold it in your hand and match it with a long series of museum specimens—like a woman matching ribbons at a drygoods counter.

So forget the subspecies. And remember that in all the continent there are a total of 650 species of birds. But if you have a nodding acquaintance with 150 or 200, less than the number in the pages of this book, you can boast that you are rather well-informed about birds.

# II

## WHAT TO LOOK FOR

A generation ago most bird books were written by museum men. So when I started to watch birds I found the usual cumbersome descriptions by which scientists describe the dead birds that lie in the long trays of their study collections. Instead of saying merely that the Robin was "a gray-backed bird with a rusty breast" they described it in minutest detail, including the white spots about the eye and the streaked throat.

In fairness to these research men who stand at the threshold of knowledge, it must be admitted that their work is fundamental. A systematic account is important when a creature is first introduced to the scientific world. Then we, who act as interpreters, can go ahead. We can then describe what the bird looks like when it is alive.

Color is the first thing many of us use when we identify flowers, but bird books arranged by color have not been too successful. It is true that we notice color first when we see a Warbler or a Tanager, but we never compare a reddish Duck with a reddish Sparrow. Rather, we first place them in their families, and then run them down by their "field marks."

It is the purpose of this book to point out (as in this section) what to look for when you see a bird, then to introduce you to the families or groups of birds, and to help you know the more well-marked species, and to point out where to find them. I have omitted the less obvious birds and the rare ones. This booklet includes about one-half of the species found in the East (or about a third of those found in North America). This is a good start, but you will, of course, want to go further. A FIELD GUIDE TO THE BIRDS is complete and includes *all* the birds found east of the Great Plains. Many are shown in color, and their songs and ranges are given. A FIELD GUIDE TO WESTERN BIRDS covers similarly the western states.

## WHAT IS ITS SIZE?

Size in inches is tricky to guess at. Use as a measuring stick some familiar bird such as a Sparrow, Robin, Pigeon, or Crow—(slightly smaller than an English Sparrow; a trifle longer than a Robin, etc.).

## WHAT IS ITS SHAPE?

Is it chunky like a Starling (left) or slender like a Cuckoo (right)?

What are its wings like? Are they pointed like those of a Swallow (left, below), or rounded like those of a Bob-white (center)?

Is it a long-legged bird, like the Yellow-legs, above?

Does it have a long bill or a short one? Is its bill thin like that of a Wren, thick like that of a Sparrow or does it have some other shape?

Does it have a crest or a top-knot (above)?

Is its tail long like that of a Mockingbird (1), medium-length like that of a Robin (2), or short like that of a Meadowlark (3)?

Is its tail *forked* like that of a Barn Swallow (1), *notched* like a Tree Swallow's (2), *square-tipped* like a Cliff Swallow's (3), *round-tipped* like a Jay's (4), or *pointed* like a Mourning Dove's (5)?

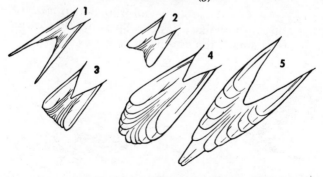

## HOW DOES IT ACT?

Does it cock its tail *up* the way a Wren often does, **or** does it hold it *down* like a Flycatcher?

Does it wag its tail?

Does it sit on an exposed perch, dart out after an insect and return? If so, it is probably a Flycatcher, although other birds act this way at times.

Does it climb trees? If so, does it climb upwards in *spirals* like a Creeper; in jerks like a Woodpecker, using its tail as a brace; or does it go down headfirst like a Nuthatch?

Does it feed on the ground, and if so, does it *walk* like a Blackbird, or *hop* like a Jay or a Sparrow? Does it rummage about among the dead leaves?

18

When we see a waterbird the things to notice are:
Does it swim? If so, does it dive like a Loon or one of the deep water Ducks, or does it dabble and tip up like a "puddle Duck"?

Does it take off from the water like a heavily-laden seaplane, spattering as it goes along, or, like a helicopter, does it clear the water in one jump?

Does it hover in one spot like a Kingfisher, or Tern (right), then dive headfirst into the water?

Does it wade? Is it a large long-legged wader like a Heron that spends much of its time standing motionless, or does it run along the muddy margin like a Sandpiper or a Plover? If it is one of the latter, does it probe the mud with its bill or does it pick at things? Does it "teeter" or "bob"?

## HOW DOES IT FLY?

Does it *undulate* (dip up and down) like a Goldfinch (below) or a Flicker?

Does it have a *straight* arrow-like flight like a Dove (below), a Starling or a Duck?

Does it fly *erratically*, lurching this way and that, like a Nighthawk?

Does it *skim* like a Swallow or a Tern?

Does it *soar* like a Gull (below) or a Hawk?

Does it beat its wings *slowly* like a Heron, or *rapidly* like a Songbird or a Duck?

Does it progress with an even wing-beat or with several flaps and a sail?

Does it travel in flocks?

## WHAT ARE ITS "FIELD MARKS"?

Some birds we can identify by color alone. If we see a small bird that appears to be all yellow, the chances are it is a Yellow Warbler. If it has a yellow body and black wings it is a Goldfinch. If it is red with black wings it is a Scarlet Tanager, and if it is red all over, with a crest, it is a Cardinal.

But most birds are not that easy. Color is often very useful, but the most important aids are what we call "field marks," which are, in effect, the "trade marks of Nature." On the following pages are some of the most useful points to look for.

Is the breast *plain* (unmarked) as in a Cuckoo (left), *spotted* as in a Wood Thrush (upper right), or *streaked* or *striped* as in a Brown Thrasher (below)?

Does the tail have a "flash pattern"? Does it have a *band* at the tip like the tail of the Kingbird (left), *white spots* like the tail of the Towhee (center), or *white sides* as in the Meadowlark (right)?

Does the bird have a light *rump-patch* like the Cliff Swallow below? The Marsh Hawk, Flicker, Myrtle Warbler and others are quickly identified by their rump-patches.

Do the wings have light *wing-bars,* or are they plain?
The presence or absence of these bars is very important
in such groups as the Warblers, Vireos and Flycatchers.

Does the bird have a *stripe* over the eye (1), or a *ring*
around the eye (2)? Is the crown *striped* (3) or is there a
*patch* on the crown (4)?

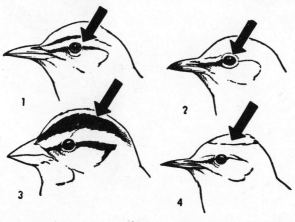

The wings of water birds are very important. Notice whether they have light *patches* (1) or *stripes* (2), are *solidly colored* (3) or have *black tips* (4).

## VOICE

Many of the keenest bird watchers I know depend more on their ears than on their eyes. Some find 90 per cent of their birds that way. On their walks they pause every few minutes and listen intently, for just as the voice of a friend can be recognized in the next room, so can the notes of a hidden bird be identified. It isn't easy to learn bird voices from the printed page. It is simpler to go with someone who can tell you what they are. But in our town I knew of no such person, and when I heard a strange song, I had to stalk the bird until I could get a good look at it. It was the hard way, but I learned them well.

Chicadees, Whip-poor-wills, Phoebes, and Bob-whites say their names plainly. Catbirds mew as Catbirds should. Ovenbirds chant *teacher, teacher, teacher* and Yellow-throats sing *witchity witchity witchity witch* just as the bird guides say they do, but most bird voices are not so simple. Song descriptions in the books vary so much that one would think they could not possibly represent the same melody. For example, the White-throated Sparrow whistles several thin icy notes which New Englanders often interpret as "Old Sam Peabody, Peabody, Peabody." Canadians insist they sound like "Sweet Canada, Canada, Canada," and one romantic writer interpreted the pensive strain as "Here comes the Bride"!

Space does not permit analyzing songs in this booklet, but I have described them in my FIELD GUIDES. Advanced students should investigate A GUIDE TO BIRD SONGS by Aretas Saunders. The easiest way of all to learn songs is by actual sound recordings. AMERICAN BIRD SONGS published by the Comstock Publishing Co., of Ithaca, New York, is an album of seventy-two songs recorded on six double-disc records. Full-bodied songs like those of the Thrushes record superbly and where it might take you years to master them otherwise, you can learn the distinctions in an evening by playing the records over and over. The high sibilant voices of Warblers do not always record as well.

## WHERE IS IT FOUND?

The Meadowlark and the Flicker are both brown birds. They are about the same size, but one lives in the fields, the other among the trees. You would never expect to see a Meadowlark in the woods, although the Flicker might leave its grove of trees to dig up an ant's nest at the edge of a field. Each species has its special place, or "habitat." The experienced bird watcher can look at a woodland, a meadow, or a swamp, and can predict almost exactly what he will find there. Habitats are discussed later in the book (Section IV, pages 137 to 152). Birds also have geographic limits, beyond which they are not found. The "ranges" of some birds like the Barn Owl or Mallard Duck are almost world-wide. Many birds such as the familiar Robin or Song Sparrow range from coast to coast, while a few species are confined almost to a single state. Most of the birds in this book are of wide distribution in the United States unless it is indicated otherwise.

## WHEN IS IT FOUND?

It helps a great deal to know the seasons in which to expect certain birds. In the East there are five kinds of Brown Thrushes. They all go through Washington, D. C., but *ordinarily* the Wood Thrush is the only one of the five you would expect to see near the Nation's Capital during the summer months (although Veeries have nested in Rock Creek Park). In the winter, the only likely species is the Hermit Thrush. During early May and again in the fall the other Thrushes pass through on their way to and from their more northern homes. A local list of the birds, such as the Audubon Society of the District of Columbia publishes, tells you these things. Find out from your nearest bird club or museum whether there is a similar publication for your locality. Many bird watchers mark on the margins of their FIELD GUIDES the birds that are found in their locality and the dates when they might be expected.

# III

## THE FAMILIES OF BIRDS

### LOONS

The laugh of a Loon on a northern lake is like the mirth of a maniac. Loons are larger than Ducks and, unlike them, have pointed bills. They are built like torpedoes for submarine diving, and their feet, like propellers, are placed so close to the tail that a Loon must taxi for a distance before getting into the air. Once aloft, it looks hunchbacked, with its neck drooping a bit and the big feet sticking out behind like a rudder.

#### Common Loon

To most people there is only one Loon, the Common Loon, shown here, a bird with a checkerboard pattern which it loses in winter (dark above, light below). There are two smaller kinds, the Red-throated Loon (both coasts), with a rusty throat, and the Pacific Loon (Pacific coast), with a gray hind-neck, but they are mostly seen in winter when they lack these trade marks. Then it is a matter for the experts.

*Horned Grebe*
*Summer*

*Winter*

*Pied-billed Grebe*
*Summer*

## GREBES

These are the "Hell-Divers," little Duck-like birds with small heads and thin necks. They look almost tailless. Unlike Ducks their bills are pointed and their feet instead of being webbed are *lobed* (inset-above). Grebes are such poor and reluctant fliers that we don't often see them in the air. Of the half dozen U. S. species the two shown here are the most widespread and familiar.

### Pied-Billed Grebe

The Grebe that most people see, a little brown *chicken-billed* diver (smaller than a Duck) that dives in the muddy ponds and pops up unexpectedly. The black spot across the bill is a good mark in summer.

### Horned Grebe

The little Grebe of the bays, big lakes and the ocean. It has a small *pointed* bill, *buffy eartufts* in spring, and a black and white pattern in winter. The Eared Grebe of the West is very much like it.

28

## SHEARWATERS

The beginner is not likely to run across a Shearwater. I went ten years before I saw my first one. Not that they are rare; large flocks cruise both coasts each year, but they keep so far off-shore that you must take a boat to find them.

The four Atlantic Coast Shearwaters and the six Pacific species are described in detail in the FIELD GUIDES. Some, like the Sooty Shearwater (both coasts), are dusky all over; others are white below like the Greater Shearwater (Atlantic), shown above (right). Shearwaters look like smallish Gulls, but have "tubed noses." Their stiff-winged flight—several flaps and a sail—barely clearing the waves, makes them look quite unlike the Gulls.

## PETRELS

If you take a boat to sea in the summertime, or travel on an ocean liner, you will see Wilson's Petrel (left, above), a small *black* bird about the size of a Martin with a *white rump*. It likes to flit in the wake of ships. Leach's Petrel nests on the Maine Coast, but is seldom seen abroad during the daytime. Sailors call Petrels "Mother Carey's Chickens."

## PELICANS

"A wonderful bird is the Pelican." Even if you live in Boston, Baltimore or Buffalo, where Pelicans are never seen, you would know one in a moment by its huge bill. These ponderous birds can float as lightly as a schooner, or glide as smoothly as a Gull, with their long bills resting comfortably on their curved necks. They often fly in lines, and play "follow-my-leader," flapping and sailing in rhythm. There are two species. The best known is the Brown Pelican shown here. Found on the seacoasts of the southern states it is familiar to everyone who visits Florida or California. This dark bird with a wingspread of 6½ feet is never found inland, but its larger relative the White Pelican often is, particularly west of the Mississippi.

In the background (above) is a Man-o'-war-bird (spread 7½ ft.), which some people call "Frigate Pelican." Long of wing and scissor-tailed it lives in the Florida Keys and throughout tropic oceans. (*See* page 86.)

## GANNETS

On four rocky islands in the Gulf of St. Lawrence live 28,000 Gannets (above, left). In migration and winter they can be seen beyond the surf along the Atlantic rim of the United States. Twice the size of Herring Gulls, adults are snow white with much black at the ends of the wings. Their tails are *pointed,* and their big bills point toward the water. They wheel in wide circles high above the waves and plunge headfirst with a splash. Young birds are dark but can be told by their pointed shape and Gannet actions. Gannets are purely accidental inland.

## JAEGERS

Jaegers (above, right) are strictly sea birds, but look more like Hawks (they even have a hook at the end of the bill). They act like birds of prey too, chasing the Gulls and Terns. The outstanding features are *two long central tail feathers* and a *flash of white* in the wing quills. Jaegers keep well offshore and for this reason are rarely seen by most bird watchers. As the three kinds are often very hard to tell apart, I am again referring you to the FIELD GUIDES.

## CORMORANTS

Fishermen call Cormorants "old black Shags." When we approach one as it stands atop a buoy with its wings held "spread-Eagle," like laundry hung out to dry, it shoves off and drops almost to the water before it gets underway. The fishermen tell us that the Shag must wet its tail before it can fly.

If we see, flying over the waves, a long string of dusky birds, larger than Ducks, the chances are they are Cormorants. Some people mistake their single-file flocks for Geese, but Geese are noisy, Cormorants silent. They are blacker than Loons, especially the adults, which are black below as well as above. At close range they show an orange-yellow throat pouch. On the water they swim low and can be told from Loons by their blacker look, snakier necks and the way they point their bills upwards at an angle. *See* Water Silhouettes, page 163.

The Double-crested Cormorant shown here is the only widespread species. It is found inland and on both coasts. There are two other common species on the Pacific side. In the swamps of the South lives another Cormorant-like bird, the Water Turkey. It is much snakier-looking, with large pale patches in its wings.

## HERONS

To some people, every long-legged wader is a "Crane," but as a matter of fact, there are very few places east of the Mississippi where one can see a real Crane. What is usually meant is a *Heron*. Bitterns and Egrets belong to the Heron family, but Cranes are not at all related *(see page 36)*.

The gangly Herons wade in the shallows, and stand motionless for minutes at a time, waiting for a fish or a frog which they spear with a lightning thrust of their sharp bills. They can stretch their necks so they are as long as their legs, or they can fold them in so that their heads rest on their shoulders as the wading Heron, above, is doing. When they fly they tuck their collapsible necks into an S curve, and their long legs trail behind. Cranes, on the other hand, fly with their necks stretched full length as shown in the right-hand bird, above. The other three birds are Great Blue Herons.

1. **Green Heron** (Most of U. S.)
   A small dark Heron, near the size of a Crow with rather short legs. This is the most familiar Heron inland in the Northeast. (*See* page 77.)

2. **Black-crowned Night Heron** (Most of U. S.)
   A chunky, short-legged Heron; black-backed and whitish below. Young birds are brown with light spots, and resemble Bitterns. Its note *quok!,* is often heard at night.

3. **Great Blue Heron** (Entire U. S.)
   Four feet tall, and gray, this big familiar Heron is often mistakenly called a "Crane."

4. **American Egret** (Entire Southern U. S.)
   Tall and white, but not quite as tall as the Great Blue Heron, the American Egret is often called the "White Crane." It differs from other white Herons in having a *yellow bill.* A few wander north in summer. Even more numerous in parts of the South is the Snowy Egret which is much smaller (size of a Little Blue Heron). It is white with *yellow feet* ("golden slippers").

5. **Little Blue Heron** (Southeastern U. S.)
   A very dark (almost blackish) medium-sized Heron with slender dark legs. Although it lives mostly in the south, a few wander north every summer. Young birds are white and look like small Egrets, but have neither yellow feet nor yellow bills as have the Egrets. A dark Heron that looks like a Little Blue Heron with a *white belly* is the Louisiana Heron.

6. **American Bittern** (Entire U. S.)
   A chunky *brown* Heron that shows black wing-tips when it flies. It often stands quietly in the marsh and escapes notice by pointing its bill to the sky and simulating the reeds. (*See* page 88.) The Least Bittern that hides in the cattails is tiny (size of a Meadowlark) and has large buffy wing-patches. (*See* page 77.)

*Wood Ibis*

*Sandhill Crane*

*White Ibis*

## OTHER LONG-LEGGED BIRDS

Most people do not know we have a native Stork in America, but the WOOD IBIS of the southern states is not really an Ibis at all. It belongs to the Stork family (*Ciconiidae*). It is the size of a Great Blue Heron, with a *naked gray head,* a white body, and much black in the spread wings. White Herons have no black in the wings. Both the Wood Ibis and the true Ibises fly with their necks stretched full length like the Cranes. Only Herons have the habit of doubling their neck in a loop.

The WHITE IBIS, abundant in some of the ricefields and marshes of the southeastern states, is a true Ibis. It is much smaller than a Wood Ibis, with a *red face* and a curved Curlew-like bill.

The SANDHILL CRANE is best known to people who live on the prairies. It is as tall as a Great Blue Heron, but is built more sturdily and has a *bald red* forehead and a tuft of long feathers that curl over the tail. It flies with neck outstretched.

## GEESE

Few men have souls so dead that they will not bother to look up when they hear the barking of wild Geese. For Geese symbolize the mystery of migration more than any other birds, and as harbingers of spring, they are second only to the Robin.

Ducks, Geese and Swans belong to the same family of birds. Geese are more *terrestrial* than Ducks, however; that is, they spend more of their time on land, where they graze in the grassy marshes and the stubble fields. Many kinds fly in orderly formation like squadrons of aircraft, either in wedges or in long stringy lines. Unlike aircraft, they shift formation more frequently. Ducks do not "talk" much while they are flying, but Geese incessantly honk or gabble to each other. Another way in which they differ from Ducks is that the sexes are alike at all times, whereas male Ducks are usually much more strikingly patterned than their drab mates. Most Geese are larger and more heavy-bodied than Ducks. Their necks are longer too, but not so long as those of the Swans.

## Canada Goose

This is the "wild Goose" that everyone knows, the big "honker" whose V, pointing like a compass-needle to the north, marks the coming of spring. Identify it by the *black stocking* on its neck and the white cheek patch. Found throughout the entire continent, it comes in various sizes. Some western races are no larger than the Snow Goose, opposite. (*See* page 76.)

Along the seacoast one sometimes sees another "black-stockinged" Goose, the Brant. Hardly larger than a Duck, it is the least land-loving of the Geese. Instead of grazing in the marshes it "tips-up" in the salt water for eel-grass and other water weeds. Its small size, black chest and a white patch on the neck are its marks.

West of the Mississippi there is a gray-brown Goose that lacks the "black stocking" of the familiar "honker." It is the White-fronted Goose and its trade marks are a white patch near its nose and black marks on its underparts which give it the sportsman's name of "speckle-belly."

## Snow Goose

Although the Snow Goose is not known as well as the "honker," there are more of them left in America today. Most of them live west of the Mississippi. They are local in the East. Flocks which often number thousands look like snow flakes in the sky. The black wing tips of Snow Geese distinguish them from the Swans. (*See* page 95.)

## Blue Goose

Seldom seen except on the prairies, when in great flocks it makes the long hop from the Arctic to the Gulf Coast of Louisiana, the Blue Goose can be told by its white head. This feature is responsible for its very appropriate nickname of "Eagle Goose." In its large flocks there is almost invariably a liberal sprinkling of Snow Geese.

Blue Goose

Canada Goose

Snow Goose

39

*Whistling Swan*

*Mute Swan*

## SWANS

Everyone knows what a Swan looks like, for he has surely watched one float like a vision on a park lake, or seen its image in the fairy tale book about the ugly duckling, or at least on the wrapper of a cake of soap. With necks even longer than those of Geese—as long, in fact, as their bodies—these immense white waterfowl are among the largest of all North American birds.

### Whistling Swan

This is our only common species, and it is common only in a few places during migration and winter (coast from Maryland to North Carolina, Great Lakes, Great Salt Lake, and central California). It can be told from the ordinary park Swan (Mute Swan) by its *black bill.*

### Mute Swan

Brought from Europe to some of the big estates, the Mute Swan can now be found wild on Long Island, the Hudson River, and the New Jersey Coast. It can be recognized by its *orange bill* which has a black *knob* near the forehead.

## DUCKS

Some Ducks dive deep, others cannot dive at all. The divers (which we call *Bay* or *Sea Ducks*) have their legs placed so close to their tails that they must run and spatter for a long way before they can gain the air. (*See* page 19.) Ducks that dabble and tip up-side-down for their food (Marsh Ducks) can launch into full flight with one jump. Anatomically there is another good distinction. The hind toe of a Diving Duck has a lobe or flap like a little paddle. This the Marsh Ducks lack. See below.

Besides these two sub-families of Ducks there are *Mergansers,* which have spike-like beaks with saw-toothed edges for holding fish, and the *Ruddy Duck,* a dumpy little fellow with eighteen or twenty long stiff tail feathers.

On the following pages I have shown many of the Ducks, but not all of them—and only the males. For a start, this is sufficient. The females can usually be told by the males they associate with. The FIELD GUIDES go into it completely, showing both sexes, on the water, in the air, and overhead. Sportsmen must know the overhead patterns, particularly, if they would avoid shooting species protected by law.

All of the species shown here, except for the Black Duck, are widespread and can be found from the Atlantic Coast to the Pacific states.

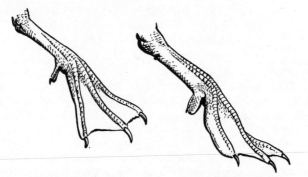

**Foot of Dabbling Duck (left); Diving Duck (right)**

## MARSH DUCKS (Dabbling Ducks)

### 1. Wood Duck

This, the most beautiful Duck in the world, is now protected by law. Its bizarre face pattern and deep rainbow iridescence distinguish it when close, but to avoid shooting the bird, sportsmen must recognize it quickly in flight by its white belly; dusky wings and long dark tail.

### 2. Black Duck

Found only east of the Rockies, the Black Duck looks like a very dark female Mallard. Its body is *dusky brown;* its head paler. When it flies it flashes *white* under the wings.

### 3. Baldpate

The shining *white crown* gives the Baldpate its name. "Widgeon" is the name the gunners use.

### 4. Mallard

This, the most widespread Duck in the world, is the ancestor of most domestic Ducks and looks just like the "puddle ducks" in the parks. Its field marks are a *green head* and *white neck ring.* (*See* page 80.)

### 5. Blue-winged Teal

A pint-sized Duck, easily recognized by a white crescent on its face and large pale patches on its wings. Another species, the Green-winged Teal, has darker wings with metallic green patches.

### 6. Pintail

The most streamlined Marsh Duck. It has a long pin-pointed tail and a thin neck with a white stripe running from it onto the side of the head.

### 7. Shoveller

It has the wing-pattern of a Blue-winged Teal and the green head of a Mallard, but its big soup-straining bill is its trade-mark.

## BAY AND SEA DUCKS (Diving Ducks)

**1. Goldeneye**

A white-bodied Duck with a *round white spot* before its eye. It whistles with its wings as it flies.

**2. Buffle-head**

A little half-pint of a Duck with a white cap on its head. It looks very white when swimming.

**3. Canvasback**

A white Duck with a rusty-red head and a *long* patrician profile. A similar species is the Redhead, now grown quite scarce due to too much hunting pressure. It is gray with a round rusty head.

**4. Scaup Duck**

At a distance these Ducks which often flock in great rafts look black at both ends and white in the middle. Two kinds are recognized by experts: the Greater and Lesser Scaup.

**5. Old-squaw**

A smart-looking Sea Duck with much white on its body, and *solid dark wings* in flight. It is the only Sea Duck with a needle-tail.

**6. White-winged Scoter**

The Scoters are the coal-black Ducks that gunners call "Sea Coots." They are most often seen on salt water. This species, which seems to be the commonest of the three, has a white square on each wing.

**7. Surf Scoter**

This species, nicknamed the "Skunk-head Coot," has white patches on its head. A third species, the American Scoter, is all black except for an orange-yellow patch on its bill. Gunners sometimes call it "Butter-nosed Coot." (*See* page 78.)

## MERGANSERS (Fish Ducks)

There are three Mergansers. All have slender bills with toothed edges instead of flat bills (see above). When a Merganser flies it holds its bill, head, neck and body in a horizontal line.

### Red-breasted Merganser

The common salt water Merganser (found on lakes too), sports a wispy crest and a white collar. (*See* page 78.)

### American Merganser

The one so often seen on rivers in the winter. It is long and white with a dark head and red bill.

### Hooded Merganser

This dark-bodied Merganser, which has a fan-like white crest, likes wooded ponds.

## RUDDY DUCK

The little Ruddy Duck is in a subfamily by itself. It boasts more nicknames than any other Duck, is the only one that cannot walk on land, and its spiky tail (which has 18 or 20 feathers) is often cocked over its back like a Wren's. In summer plumage with its rusty body and white cheeks it is unmistakable. (*See* page 87.)

Red-Breasted
Merganser

American
Merganser

Hooded
Merganser

Ruddy Duck

# SILHOUETTES OF THREE BASIC TYPES OF HAWKS

**Falcons**
Long Tail, Long Pointed Wings

**Accipiters (Bird Hawks)**
Long Tail, Rounded Wings

**Buteos (Soaring Hawks)**
Broad Tail, Broad Wings

# HAWKS

During the recent war, those of us who were in the army, and those civilians who volunteered as plane spotters, learned how to tell enemy planes from friendly planes by their silhouettes. We were taught how to identify a British Spitfire from a German Messerschmitt when it was hardly more than a speck in the sky. An expert could tell any one of dozens of fighter planes and bombers at a quick glance.

The same principles are used by the Hawk watchers who search the sky at Hawk Mountain in eastern Pennsylvania on October Sundays, or the bird recorders who visit Cape May Point to watch the autumn flight. They contend that planes are merely wood and fabric replicas of Hawks and that to recognize either planes or Hawks one looks for the same points—shape of wings, shape of tail, "fuselage" and "dihedral." Certain birds of prey, like the Falcons, might be compared to fighter planes or dive bombers. Some Hawks are power fliers, equipped with jet propulsion, while others are essentially gliders. Eagles might be classed as "flying fortresses."

In identifying a Hawk, first place it, if you can, in one of the three basic groups shown on the page opposite. This is a convenient simplification, but sometimes a round-winged *Buteo* will close the tips of its wings in order to descend, or a sharp-winged Falcon might spread the feathers of its wing-tips so as to take full advantage of the lifting air currents. Hawks, then, can change their "sail surface," so as to rise or drop, but on the whole the wing shapes shown here are very practical.

NOTE: Today most well-informed sportsmen and farmers no longer kill Hawks, for they now know that the birds of prey are not detrimental to their sport, and that they play a valuable role in keeping the balance of nature. Only those who are ignorant and destructive shoot them, but unfortunately there are still so many people who are biologically illiterate that some birds of prey have grown scarce.

## FALCONS

These are the fast aircraft among birds of prey—more streamlined than the others with *long pointed wings* and *longish tails.* The gentle little *Kestrel,* however, is like a helicopter and often hovers in one spot on rapidly beating wings. When it spots a grasshopper or a mouse it quickly makes a pin-point landing. The *Merlin* is more like a fast little pursuit plane, but the *Peregrine,* the Falcon made famous by medieval knights and falconers, is a dive bomber, scoring direct hits upon its prey while diving 200 miles per hour. Systematic ornithologists do not classify the Falcons with the Hawks but place them in a separate family.

### Kestrel or Sparrow Hawk

Slightly larger than a Robin this small rusty Hawk has a *rufous-red tail.*

### Merlin or Pigeon Hawk

Slightly larger than a Jay. It is dusky with a *banded gray tail.*

### Peregrine or Duck Hawk

This prince of predators is nearly the size of a Crow, has a light breast and black mustaches.

Falcons have long pointed wings, longish tails and broad shoulders.

Peregrine
or Duck Hawk

Kestrel
or Sparrow Hawk

Merlin
or Pigeon Hawk

## ACCIPITERS (Bird Hawks)

These are the only true *Hawks* if we accept the old English definition, for in England they always speak of the others as Buzzards, Harriers, and Falcons. Accipiters specialize in hedge-hopping and dodging through the woods. Their tails are long, and their wings *short and rounded,* so as to take up less room when they maneuver among the trees. Country folk call them "Blue-Darters" (adults have blue-gray backs). There are three species, but the big Goshawk of the north is not often encountered by the beginner.

### Sharp-shinned Hawk

A small Accipiter, not much larger than a Robin, with a *square-tipped* or *notched* tail.

### Cooper's Hawk

Almost identical to the Sharp-shin, but Crow-sized with a *rounded* tail.

Accipiters have short rounded wings,
long tails, and small heads.

## HARRIER (Marsh Hawk)

There is only one Harrier and it is easy to recognize. Whether a pale gray male or a brown female, it always shows a *white rump spot* as it flies low over the meadows. The tail is long and the wings are too, but not pointed like those of the Falcon.

*Sharp=shinned Hawk*

*Cooper's Hawk*

*Harrier or Marsh Hawk*

## BUTEOS (Soaring or Buzzard Hawks)

There are the big soaring Hawks, larger than Crows, that wheel in wide circles in the blue, riding the thermals of warm air that bubble up from the earth. We cannot see these thermals, but the Hawks can feel them in their wings.

The birds of this group have *broad wings* and *broad rounded tails* which they often spread like a fan. The adults of three of the best-known species are described here. Young birds are much trickier and often stump the experts. They are described and illustrated in color on page 54 of the FIELD GUIDE.

### Broad-winged Hawk (Dry eastern woodlands)

The *wide* white tail bands make this chunky Hawk easy to identify. It sometimes migrates in large flocks.

### Red-shouldered Hawk (Wet eastern woodlands)

Rusty shoulders are its mark. Unlike those of the Broad-winged Hawk, its white tail bands are *narrow*.

### Red-tailed Hawk (Coast to coast)

A glimpse of its bright rusty red tail is all that is necessary to name this large Hawk. It can sometimes be seen perched on a bare tree near the road.

Buteos are **chunky**, have broad wings and broad tails.

*Broad-winged Hawk*

*Red-shouldered Hawk*

*Red-tailed Hawk*

55

Osprey
Bald Eagle

## EAGLES

Actually, Eagles are nothing more than large Hawks very closely related to the *Buteos*. If we are to give them any distinction it is that they are larger, with longer wings and larger beaks. There are two species in America. No one could mistake our national emblem the Bald Eagle (above), with its white head and white tail. Young birds, however, have dark heads and tails and are much like the Golden Eagle of the western mountains. (*See* FIELD GUIDE.) The Bald Eagle is a fish-eater, so it usually lives close to water, ranging along the coast and the shores of large lakes and rivers.

## OSPREYS

"Fish Hawks," as they are sometimes called, are like small Eagles, but have *clear white* underparts.

I have often seen the Bald Eagle, Osprey and Turkey Vulture in the air at the same time. If not too distant they can be identified by their pattern, but there is another very good way: An Eagle soars on *flat* wings; an Osprey with a *kink* or *crook;* and a Turkey Vulture with a *dihedral*. Next time you see a big bird a mile away try this "plane-spotting" technique. An Eagle and an Osprey are shown soaring in the distance behind the Vulture on the opposite page. (*See* page 84.)

Osprey

Bald Eagle

Turkey Vulture

## VULTURES

In the early morning, groups of Vultures sit hunched upon the branches of dead trees waiting for the sun to cause thermals of warm air to rise. Then they launch forth to climb and soar on these "breezes that blow upwards." Vultures are the greatest gliders on earth. Their wings have a span nearly that of an Eagle, and to take full advantage of the air currents, they spread wide the feathers at the tips of their wings like fingers. There are two kinds of these small-headed eaters of carrion. Some people call them "Buzzards."

### Turkey Vulture

This, the most widespread Vulture (shown above), is sometimes found north to Canada. It has two-toned wings, a rather longish tail, and a red head. It soars with a dihedral (which means that it holds its wings above the horizontal). The other species, the Black Vulture, is more southern. It flaps much more, shows a *white patch* near the wing-tip, and has a *very stubby tail*. It is not nearly so buoyant in the air as its red-headed relative. (*See* page 86.)

# CHICKEN-LIKE BIRDS

Grouse, Quail and Pheasants scratch for a living and, as you might suspect from their appearance, are wild cousins of the biddies of the barnyard. A small Asiatic member of the Pheasant family, the Red Junglefowl, which looks very much like a Bantam, is the ancestor of all domestic Chickens.

There are about twenty members of the order *Galliformes* in North America. On the page opposite are shown the most widespread Grouse, the most familiar Quail and the one introduced species of Pheasant. I have omitted the Turkey, as the wild bird is, in general appearance, like the familiar barnyard Turkey except for the rusty tips on its tail feathers.

### Ruffed Grouse

This Chicken-like bird is found in woodlands across the northern tier of states from coast to coast. It might be either rusty or gray, but its *fan-like tail* with a black band near the tip is its trade mark. Do not call it *Ruffled* Grouse. In the midland grass country lives the Prairie Chicken, a heavily barred Grouse with a *short dark tail.*

### Bob-white

Small and chunky, the Bob-white could hardly be confused with anything else, except, possibly, a Meadowlark. Its bright rusty color, striped head and short black tail identify it. This is the only Quail in the eastern and central states. The common Quail in the West is the California Quail. It is gray with a nodding top-knot. *See* Roadside Silhouettes, page 157.

### Pheasant

In farming country north of Mason and Dixon's Line struts the gorgeous Pheasant. Its sweeping tail and the ring on its neck quickly identify it. Female Pheasants are brown, but can be told from Grouse by their long pointed tails. (*See* page 80.)

Ruffed Grouse

Bob-white

Pheasant

*Coot*

*Florida Gallinule*

## COOTS and GALLINULES

Coots and Gallinules (above), and Rails (opposite) all belong to one family of marsh dwellers whose mysterious voices come from the reeds. Whereas Rails wade about somewhat like Shorebirds, Coots and Gallinules spend most of their time swimming. They remind us more of Ducks, from which they can be distinguished by their small heads which they pump back and forth as they swim, and their rather chicken-like bills.

### Florida Gallinule

Sooty gray with a *bright red bill*. No Duck has a red bill.

### Coot

Slaty gray with a *white bill*. No Duck has a white bill. Although Gallinules stay back in the pools in the marsh most of the time, Coots often flock in the open on lakes and bays. They make hard work of flying and skitter and spatter over the water when taking off. When Coots walk along the shore notice their enormous feet. They are not webbed like those of a Duck, but are equipped with lobes or flaps on each toe. Coots therefore are good divers.

*Sora*                    *Virginia Rail*

## RAILS

Rails are often called "Marsh Hens," a very apt nickname, for they have a decidedly Chicken-like look. We hear their mysterious voices often but seldom see the birds because they are more likely to sneak away through the reeds, unobserved, than to fly. If they are so pressed that flight seems the only escape, they will jump into the air, fly feebly for a few feet, with legs dangling, and drop back into the grass. When you see a Rail notice first whether it has a short stubby bill or a long slender one. Then take note of its size.

### Sora

Small (size of Quail), gray or tan with a *short* yellow bill. It lives in fresh marshes and is the only common Rail with a short bill.

### Virginia Rail

Small (size of Quail) ; rusty with a *long bill*. It might be found either in a fresh or a salt marsh. If, in a fresh marsh, especially in the South, you see a rusty Rail that is as large as a small Chicken, it is a King Rail. If you see it in a salt marsh and it is *gray*, it is a Clapper Rail. (*See* page 76.)

## SHOREBIRDS

The Shorebirds, by which we mean the Sandpipers and Plovers, are the toughest birds of all to identify. The little Spotted Sandpiper that runs along the margins of nearly every stream and shore the length and breadth of the continent is known to everyone, and so is the Killdeer. But there are, besides these, a host of obscure waders that stop briefly on their way to and from their Arctic breeding grounds. Most of them take the coastal or the prairie flyways, but a few can be found wherever there is a bit of mud or shoreline to walk on. They are particularly puzzling in the fall.

Most Shorebirds are small or medium-sized, with slender bills for probing in the mud and water, and slender legs for wading. On the next pages are shown a few representative Plovers and Sandpipers. As I cannot possibly include all of them, I am presenting a page of basic patterns opposite. Learn these patterns and, with the help of the FIELD GUIDES, you will know the Shorebirds. But do not be discouraged if you can't master them in one season.

1. **Dark wings—whitish rump and tail**
   Yellow-legs (also Stilt Sandpiper and Wilson's Phalarope)

2. **Dark wings—white sides of tail**
   Solitary Sandpiper

3. **Dark wings—dark tail** (no pattern)
   Golden Plover (also Pectoral Sandpiper and Curlew)

4. **White wing stripe—whitish rump and tail**
   Dowitcher (also Black-bellied Plover (*see* page 79), Willet, Knot, White-rumped Sandpiper)

5. **White wing stripe—dark tail**
   Sanderling (also Spotted, Semipalmated, Least, and Red-backed Sandpipers, and others)

6. **White wing stripe—rusty tail**
   Killdeer

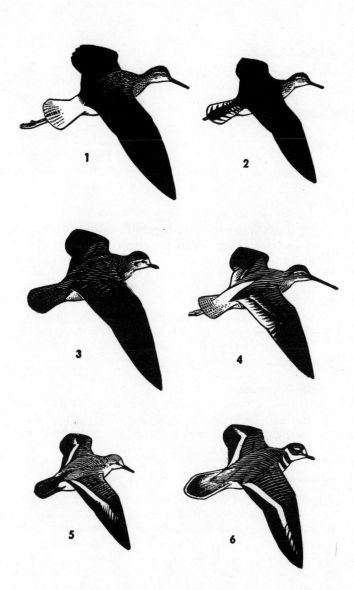

**BASIC PATTERNS OF SHOREBIRDS**

## PLOVERS

These birds of the beach are much like Sandpipers, but are stockier, with thicker necks and shorter, stouter bills. Most of them have a handsome pattern. The Turnstone belongs in a separate family.

### Killdeer

The noisy Killdeer, the best known Plover, likes fields, pastures and golf courses. The size of a Robin or larger, it has *two rings* across its breast.

### Ringed Plover (or Semipalmated Plover)

This small brown-backed Shorebird, hardly larger than a Sparrow, is known by the *single black ring* across its breast. A similar species, the Piping Plover, has a very pale back, the color of dry sand.

### Black-bellied Plover

*Black below* and pale above, the big Black-belly is a distinctive bird. In fall it loses the black on the underparts. Then it can be told by the tuft of black feathers in its "arm-pits" (under the wings).

### Ruddy Turnstone

The dumpy Turnstone can always be told by its *orange legs* and the patchy "calico" pattern as it flies away. In spring it has a rusty back and a strange black and white face pattern.

## "SNIPE"

Sportsmen once called all Sandpipers "Snipe," and considered them fair game. Today, except for Woodcock and Wilson's Snipe, most Shorebirds can not be legally taken.

The chunky Woodcock with its dead-leaf pattern and rounded wings (*see* page 88), and Wilson's Snipe, with its pointed wings and zig-zag flight, are long-billed members of the Sandpiper family. The Woodcock likes alders and moist brushy thickets, while Wilson's Snipe prefers open bogs and marshy spots.

*Wilson's Snipe*

*Woodcock*

*Black-bellied Plover*

*Ruddy Turnstone*

*Ringed Plover*

*Killdeer*

# SANDPIPERS

The thirty kinds of Sandpipers in North America are a confusing lot, but if you know the following few you can learn most of the others by means of comparison.

**1. Yellow-legs**

Gray and slender, with *bright yellow legs*. There are two species, the Greater and the Lesser Yellowlegs.

**2. Willet**

Big and gray, it leaves no doubt what it is when it opens its spectacular wings.

**3. Solitary Sandpiper**

This dark-winged bird with white sides on its tail trips along the banks of wooded ponds and streams.

**4. Dowitcher**

Unlike Wilson's Snipe, this bird prefers open mud flats. Its long bill and *white rump* are its marks.

**5. Spotted Sandpiper**

The one Sandpiper everyone sees. Constant "teetering" and round Thrush-like spots (in summer) identify it.

**6. Sanderling**

It plays tag with the waves along the beach and flashes a broad wing stripe when it flies.

**7. Semipalmated Sandpiper**

The commonest of the streaked Sparrow-sized Sandpipers that swarm the flats. They are collectively called "Peep." The Least Sandpiper is smaller, with *yellowish legs* (Semipalmated has dark legs).

# OTHER SHOREBIRDS

Besides the Sandpipers and Plovers there are three other Shorebird families: (1) Oystercatchers (southern coasts); (2) Avocets and Stilts (mostly West); and (3) Phalaropes. If a small Sandpiper alights upon the water and swims it is a Phalarope. *See* Water Silhouettes, page 163. There are three species, but the beginner is not likely to encounter them.

## GULLS

Combining the gifts of swimming and soaring, Gulls float buoyantly on the waves or glide on the breeze like a sloop before the wind. Most Gulls are larger than Pigeons with wings that are much longer in proportion. They are largely white with pearly gray backs. The young ones run to dappled browns.

The things to look for on a Gull are:

1. Its wing-tips
2. The color of its feet
3. The color of its bill

Never call them "Sea-Gulls." Call them Herring Gulls, Laughing Gulls, or whatever they may be. "Sea-Gull" is inappropriate, for flocks can even be seen on the prairies. Below are the better known species:

**Herring Gull** (Inland and both coasts)
Black wing-tips and pink legs. Use this familiar Gull as the standard of comparison. (*See* page 79.)

**Ring-billed Gull** (Inland and both coasts)
Like a small buoyant Herring Gull but with a black ring on its bill and yellow-green legs.

**Great Black-backed Gull** (Mostly northeast coast)
Large with a black back and black wings.

**Laughing Gull** (Atlantic Coast only)
This small Gull with the hysterical cries has dark wings with a white border. In winter its black head turns light. On the prairies lives a similar black-headed hysterical species, Franklin's Gull. (*See* page 86.)

**Bonaparte's Gull** (Inland and both coasts)
Very small with a long white triangle toward the end of the wing. It has a black hood in spring.

There are other species besides those above, particularly along the West Coast. To identify them and the confusing young Gulls refer to the FIELD GUIDES.

Bonaparte's Gull

Ring=billed Gull

Herring Gull

Laughing Gull

Great Black=backed Gull

# TERNS

Gulls are known as the symbols of grace and maneuverability, yet they cannot compare in these attributes with their close relatives, the Terns. Most Terns can be immediately recognized as Terns by two features—a *forked tail* and a *black cap*. In fall and winter the cap is shoved back over the ears and a white forehead shows.

As befits their more completely aerial life (they do not even swim), Terns are more streamlined than Gulls. Their wings are narrower, their tails longer. Their sharper bills are poised mosquito-wise toward the waves, and when a bird spies a fish it hovers like a Kingfisher, then plunges headfirst.

A dozen Terns nest in the United States. Below are the ones most likely to be encountered. The fantastic Skimmer belongs to a separate family.

**Common Tern** (Atlantic Coast and inland lakes)
Half the size of a Gull, it has an *orange-red* bill with *black tip*. In the West and in the South a bird that answers this description is more likely to be the very similar Forster's Tern. (*See* Field Guides.)

**Least Tern** (Both coasts and Lower Mississippi Valley)
A tiny Tern with a *yellow* bill.

**Royal Tern** (Only coasts of southern states)
As large as a Ring-billed Gull with a shaggy crest and a large orange bill. If you see such a bird in the northern states it is undoubtedly a Caspian Tern. The Royal Tern is never found inland or north. (*See* page 79.)

**Black Tern** (Inland and both coasts)
Unmistakable in spring with its *black body* and gray wings, but confusing in the fall. Then it is dark above, and white below with a patched head.

**Black Skimmer** (Atlantic Coast only)
This bizarre bird, often found with the Terns, is black above, with a long *unequal red bill*. (*See* page 79.)

A Typical Tern
(Common Tern)

Common

Least

Royal

Black

Black Skimmer

*Mourning Dove*

## DOVES

The common ordinary park Pigeon that struts like an exhibitionist before his lady love lived on cliffs by the sea in the old world, and was called the Rock Dove. The buildings of the big cities are man-made cliffs in a sense, so it is not surprising that Pigeons, escaped from domestication, have gone wild in cities everywhere.

Throughout the world there are hundreds of kinds of Pigeons and Doves (the terms are interchangeable), and they are characterized by their plump bodies and small slender Plover-like bills. Although a number of kinds live along our southern border, the only one besides the Domestic Pigeon that can be found the length and breadth of the country is the Mourning Dove, shown above. It is brown, smaller than the Domestic Pigeon, and slimmer. Instead of a fan-shaped tail it has a *pointed* tail that displays large white spots when spread.

If, in summertime, you take a trip across the country from New York City to the West Coast, and back again by way of the southern states—California, Texas and Florida—you will see Mourning Doves along the roadside on more days during your journey than any other bird. (*See* Roadside Silhouettes.)

## BIRDS OF GRASSLAND

Most birds of the open country — meadows, fields, prairies—have distinctive songs, easy to remember. Some, like the DICKCISSEL (upper right) of mid-western fields, are unmusical. But their notes are unmistakable.

The BOBOLINK (center right) has an "advertising" song. The bird commands a larger audience by pouring its notes from aloft. Many open-country birds have song routines of this type.

The PIPIT (lower right), inconspicuous as it forages on the dark earth during migration, acquires a very different personality when it reaches its tundra home where it performs in spectacular flight display. Note its white outer tail feathers which suggest the Vesper Sparrow.

**73**

DICKCISSEL

BOBOLINK

PIPIT

TREE SWALLOW

CLIFF SWALLOW

ALDER FLYCATCHER

CRESTED FLYCATCHER

# THE AIR PATROL

Swallows and Flycatchers, in their endless pursuit of flying insects, use dissimilar techniques. Swallows constantly cruise, whereas Flycatchers patiently wait until an insect buzzes by, dart out, snap it up, and return to the lookout post.

The TREE SWALLOW (upper left), steely blue above and pure white below, often nests in bird boxes.

The CLIFF SWALLOW (second left), identified by its buffy rump, builds its jug of mud under the eaves of barns.

The ALDER FLYCATCHER (third left), one of several very confusing small Flycatchers, can best be separated by voice and habitat *(See, A Field Guide to the Birds).*

The CRESTED FLYCATCHER (lower left) may be spotted by its rusty tail.

**74**

# FORESTERS

Woodpeckers are the master tree surgeons, testing the diseased limbs with sharp raps of the bill and digging out the larvae of wood-boring beetles and carpenter ants. Old forests and mature groves have many more Woodpeckers than second-growth woodlots.

HAIRY WOODPECKER

The HAIRY WOOD-PECKER (upper right) is a larger, large-billed edition of the familiar Downy Woodpecker.

RED-BELLIED WOODPECKER

The RED-BELLIED WOODPECKER (center right), commonest in the South, is red-capped, zebra-backed.

The RED-COCKADED WOODPECKER (lower right), another zebra-backed Woodpecker, has a black cap, white cheeks. A bird of southern pines, it is relatively uncommon.

**75**

RED-COCKADED WOODPECKER

GADWALL

CANADA GOOSE

VIRGINIA RAIL

VIRGINIA RAIL

# BIRDS OF MARSHES

Marshes, particularly fresh-water marshes, are great havens for water-fowl. If we wish to maintain our millions of Ducks and Geese we must stop the unhappy habit of draining these wetlands.

The GADWALL (upper left), a gray Duck with a white "speculum" is common on the prairies, less common in marshes and ponds of the Atlantic Seaboard.

The CANADA GOOSE (center left), our best-known Goose in North America, is known by its black neck-stocking and white chin-strap.

The VIRGINIA RAIL (lower left), a rusty Quail-sized bird with a thin bill, gray cheeks, is more often heard than seen. The Sora Rail has a shorter, stubby bill, is not reddish.

**76**

## SWAMP BIRDS

Open wetlands blanketed with sedge or reeds are usually regarded as marshes, whereas a wetland area invaded by shrubs or trees is termed a swamp. The birds on this page could fit either category, although only the Green Heron will be found in heavily wooded swamps.

The LEAST BITTERN (upper right), the tiniest of all the Herons, is the size of a Meadowlark. It shows large buffy wing-patches when it flies.

The GREEN HERON (center right) is Crow-sized, looks quite black when flying.

The PURPLE GALLINULE (lower right), a colorful, more southern bird than the Florida Gallinule, likes waterlily-choked swamps. Note the blue forehead, yellow legs.

**77**

LEAST BITTERN

GREEN HERON

PURPLE GALLINULE

# SEA DUCKS

SURF SCOTER

During the winter months there is a greater variety of birds on salt water than in summer, largely because of the Sea Ducks which come down from the Canadian Arctic.

Long flocks of Scoters string low over the waves. Of the three species, the SURF SCOTER (upper left), black with white head-patches, is the most distinctive. The White-winged Scoter has white wing-patches; the American Scoter has no white on its all-black plumage.

Locally numerous is the RED-BREASTED MERGANSER (lower left), a fish-eating Duck. The crested green-black head, white collar and rusty breast identify the males. Females have rusty heads.

November to April are the best months for the Sea Ducks

RED-BREASTED MERGANSER

**78**

# BIRDS OF THE SHORE

The beaches and mudflats are most rewarding in late summer, August and September, although they are quite birdy any month in the year.

The KITTIWAKE (upper right), most oceanic of all the gulls, has black feet. It may occasionally be seen from the beaches.

The ROYAL TERN (second right), year-round resident of southern beaches, is a large Tern with an orange or deep yellow bill, rarely noted north of New Jersey.

The BLACK-BELLIED PLOVER (third right) is one of the easiest Shorebirds to identify when in summer dress. Grey winter plumage is more nondescript.

The BLACK SKIMMER (lower right), seldom seen away from salt water, is unmistakable in pattern and shape.

KITTIWAKE

ROYAL TERN

BLACK-BELLIED PLOVER

BLACK SKIMMER

BLUE JAY

MALLARD DUCK

# BIRDS IN WINTER

During the closing days of each year the National Audubon Society conducts a nationwide "Christmas Count." Several thousand observers in several hundred areas go all out for a count of all the birds they can find in a day within circles fifteen miles in diameter. Coastal counts are highest. The top count, 184 species, was made at Cocoa, Florida, in 1955. Counts exceeding 100 species have been made as far north as Rhode Island and Massachusetts. Inland counts are very much smaller.

The three birds shown here — BLUE JAY, MALLARD DUCK and RING-NECKED PHEASANT — are year-round residents in some localities, although the first two are highly migratory as well.

**80**

RING-NECKED PHEASANT

## VISITORS FROM THE NORTH

During the cold months in the northern states and in southern Canada, the bird-watcher looks for "Northern Finches," erratic wanderers which may put in an appearance one year and not the next. It is debatable whether food supply or some other population pressure dictates these wanderings.

The PINE GROSBEAK (upper right) is a rosy, Robin-sized Finch with a stubby bill and wing-bars.

The EVENING GROSBEAK (center right), golden with great white patches on the black wings, swarms to feeding trays when sunflower seeds are provided.

The WHITE-WINGED CROSSBILL (lower right), a shade larger than a Sparrow, may be known from the Red Crossbill by its two white wing-bars

**81**

PINE GROSBEAK

EVENING GROSBEAK

WHITE-WINGED CROSSBILL

YELLOW WARBLER

CHESTNUT-SIDED WARBLER

PRAIRIE WARBLER

PRAIRIE WARBLER

BLACK-THROATED GREEN WARBLER

# SPRING WARBLERS

When the wood Warblers surge northward in May, bird-watching reaches its yearly climax.

The YELLOW WARBLER (upper left) is the only small bird that appears to be *all* yellow. The red streaks of the male are noticeable only at close range.

The CHESTNUT-SIDED WARBLER (second left) of brushy pastures and bushy slopes has a yellow cap, chestnut flanks.

The PRAIRIE WARBLER (third left) also prefers open scrubby growth. The face pattern, side-stripes and tail-wagging habit identify it.

The BLACK-THROATED GREEN WARBLER (lower left) lives in hemlocks and other conifers. The yellow cheek, black throat, are its marks.

**82**

## MIGRATION

Of all the many things birds do, migration provokes our deepest wonder. Thousands of papers, articles and books have been written on this subject, but even to this day we still know very little about the mechanics of orientation. Just what guides these frail travellers? There are clues, but we remain baffled.

A general reference for the beginner is *The Migration of Birds* by F. C. Lincoln (Circular No. 16, U. S. Dept. of Interior, Fish and Wildlife Service, Washington, D. C.)

The INDIGO BUNTING (upper right) and the SCARLET TANAGER (center right) migrate to the tropics but the WHITE-CROWNED SPARROW (lower right) winters in the southern states.

INDIGO BUNTING

SCARLET TANAGER

WHITE-CROWNED SPARROW

OSPREY

## NESTS

A bird's nest is not a home but a cradle for its young. Most nests are used for only a single season, or for a single brood, but the OSPREY (upper left) repairs its twiggy eyrie every year and may occupy it until the bulky structure crashes to earth.

The KINGFISHER (lower left) digs a long tunnel in a sand bank and lays its white eggs in a chamber at the terminus.

An expert can recognize most nests at a glance, even without seeing the owners. For identification of nests, the two guides by Richard Headstrom are recommended: *Birds' Nests* (for use east of the 100th meridian) and *Birds' Nests of the West* (for use west of the 100th meridian). Ives Washburn, N. Y.

**84**

KINGFISHER

# PREDATION

*Predation* is the eating of one animal by another. The Osprey and the Kingfisher on the page opposite are predators on fish, while the LONG-EARED OWL (upper right) and BARN OWL (lower right) are predators on rats and mice.

Wildlife conservation does not mean destroying every Kingfisher that takes a fish or every Owl that catches a rabbit. The reaction of the the true sportsman to the Owl should be one of admiration for a fellow hunter. Predators have lived for milleniums in adjustment with the creatures they hunt. They never wipe out game, but take their allotted percentage, culling out the less wary or the unhealthy. Predators are important to the natural balance, guardians of the health and vigor of wildlife.

**85**

LONG-EARED OWL

BARN OWL

**ROUGH-LEGGED HAWK**

**TURKEY VULTURE**

**MAN-O-WAR BIRD**

**FRANKLIN'S GULL**

# FLIGHT

Birds have wings; they are not earth-bound as we are. In this lies much of their appeal.

Orville Wright once wrote: "We got plenty of flying fever from watching the birds, but we got nothing about their secret of balance." Not until the advent of the slow-motion picture have we been able to analyze with accuracy the action of a bird's wing, nor have we been able to relate subtleties of design and function. For the air-minded we recommend Storer's *The Flight of Birds* (Cranbrook Institute of Science).

The birds on this page are masters of gliding and soaring flight. They are ROUGH-LEGGED HAWK (upper left), TURKEY VULTURE (second left), MAN-O-WAR-BIRD (third left) & FRANKLIN'S GULL (lower left).

**86**

## BEHAVIOR

Why do birds behave as they do? What is the meaning of the bizarre posturings of the two ROSEATE TERNS (upper right), or of the RUDDY DUCKS (lower right)? These are obviously displays, ceremonies connected with courtship.

Few of the actions of birds can be called the product of intelligence; most of their actions seem to be rather robot-like responses to situations. Behaviorists point out that it is false to interpret bird behavior in terms of our own. They are not little human beings dressed in feathers.

As an introduction to this facet of bird-watching read chapters 7 to 10 in James Fisher's *Watching Birds* (Pelican Books) or Armstrong's *Bird Display* (Cambridge University Press).

**87**

ROSEATE TERNS

RUDDY DUCKS

BITTERN

## CONCEALING COLORATION

The BITTERN (upper left) is streaked in such a way as to disappear among the reeds. Standing motionless, bill pointed skyward, it becomes almost invisible. The WOODCOCK (lower left) has an effective dead leaf pattern.

Many sorts of birds (and mammals and insects too) have "protective" coloration. Some are countershaded; that is, they are lighter below than above, so that the shadow on the light underparts approximately matches the tone value of the upperparts. Many Sandpipers and other ground birds possess this cryptic coloration. If an irregular, bold pattern breaks up the bird's shape (such as the Killdeer's two black breast bars) we say that the bird has "ruptive" pattern.

**88**

WOODCOCK

# SNOWSUITS

The SNOWY OWL (upper right), white against white, is easily overlooked as it sits on the snow-covered dunes or among the ice-cakes by the sea edge.

The GYRFALCON (lower right), in its white color-phase, occasionally comes to us from the glaciers of Greenland. Its pointed wings, fast flight and small Hawk-like head distinguish it from the Snowy Owl.

Whereas the above two Arctic birds retain their white plumage throughout the year, the Willow Ptarmigan (a sort of Arctic Grouse) changes from rusty-brown to a patch-work of brown and white and finally to white. It is almost invisible against the snow until it flies, flashing its short black tail.

SNOWY OWL

GYRFALCON

**89**

CARDINAL

LOGGERHEAD SHRIKE

YELLOW THROATED WARBLER

CAROLINA WREN

## BIRD SONG

Why do birds sing? They apparently do not sing for the same motives we do, although a burst of song may well be an expression of emotion. It is generally agreed that the most important functions of song are to proclaim territory and invite attention from the opposite sex.

The most useful references are (1) *A Guide to Bird Songs* by Aretas A. Saunders (D. Appleton-Century Company, N. Y.), and (2) Phonograph records (for a list write the National Audubon Society, 1130 Fifth Ave., N.Y. 28, N.Y.).

On this page are shown four songsters of the southern countryside: CARDINAL (upper left), LOGGERHEAD SHRIKE (second left), YELLOW-THROATED WARBLER (third left) and CAROLINA WREN (lower left).

**90**

# WHERE THE WEST BEGINS

In dividing our country according to the distribution of plants and birds, most biologists draw the line at the 100th meridian. Westward beyond that invisible threshold many Eastern birds drop out to be replaced by Western species.

The LAZULI BUNTING (upper right), turquoise with a cinnamon breast, replaces the Indigo Bunting on brushy slopes.

The LARK BUNTING (second right), black with white wing-patches, flocks on the plains and prairies.

The LESSER PRAIRIE CHICKEN (third right), with purplish neck-sacs, lives on the southern Great Plains.

The SAGE GROUSE (lower right) is native to the sage plains of the northern Rocky Mountain region.

91

LAZULI BUNTING

LARK BUNTING

LESSER PRAIRIE CHICKEN

SAGE GROUSE

SCOTT'S ORIOLE

## DESERT BIRDS

Deserts are seldom "barren" in the biological sense. Our Sonoran Desert in southern Arizona is particularly exciting, truly a "living desert." The rich variety of birds is fairly easy to observe because of the open terrain, but go out early. During midday most desert birds take a siesta.

The SCOTT'S ORIOLE (upper left) is seldom found far from tall yuccas. Its black head and yellow underparts distinguish it from other orioles of the desert.

SCALED QUAIL

The SCALED QUAIL (center left) prefers the grassy "Upper Sonoran" desert avoids the sun-baked flats. Note its "cotton top."

The WHITE-WINGED DOVE (lower left), Mourning Dove-sized with white wing-patches, invades the cactus gardens and the lower mountain slopes.

**92**

WHITE-WINGED DOVE

# BIRDS OF WESTERN MOUNTAINS

When west of the 100th meridian, consult *A Field Guide to Western Birds* in all matters of identification. On this page are shown four of the many interesting birds of the mountains. They may wander lower in winter.

The BAND-TAILED PIGEON (upper right), similar in size and shape to the Domestic Pigeon, forages in the oaks.

The CLARK'S NUT-CRACKER (second right), a sort of Crow, lives in pines close to the timber line.

The BOHEMIAN WAXWING (third right) is a winter wanderer from Canada and Alaska.

The ROSY FINCH (lower right), high-ranging, is seen above the timber line, but may move to high plains in winter.

BAND-TAILED PIGEON

CLARK'S NUTCRACKER

BOHEMIAN WAXWING

ROSY FINCH

TRICOLORED BLACKBIRD

HEPATIC TANAGER

RUFOUS HUMMINGBIRD

CACTUS WREN

# GAY WESTERNERS

The traveller from the East finds that half the birds he sees in the West are birds he already knows.

The TRICOLORED BLACKBIRD (upper left) looks like the ordinary Red-wing except that its shoulder-patches are edged with white instead of yellow. It lives in large colonies, mostly in California.

The HEPATIC TANAGER (second left), red with a blackish bill, summers among pines in the high mountains near the Mexican border.

The RUFOUS HUMMINGBIRD (third left), bright rusty with a ruby throat, migrates north through the Pacific states, returns via the mountains.

The CACTUS WREN (lower left), largest wren, haunts the cholla gardens.

**94**

## RARE WESTERNERS

The WHITE-TAILED KITE (upper right), a Falcon-like bird, may be mistaken for a small Gull as it quarters over the meadows, hunting mice. The climate of public opinion has changed in favor of this bird and it seems to be showing an increase in California.

The ROSS'S GOOSE (lower right), like a small edition of the Snow Goose, migrates from the Canadian Arctic to the Sacramento Valley of California where small groups consort with the flocks of Snow Geese.

Both the White-tailed Kite and Ross's Goose have been known to appear far from their usual localities. Birds have wings; therefore rarities turn up. This helps make bird-watching the most popular of all outdoor hobbies.

**95**

WHITE-TAILED KITE

ROSS'S GOOSE

# VANISHING SPECIES

These are the rarest of the rare.

If the Ivory-billed Woodpecker is still with us (of this we are not certain), it is America's rarest bird. Bird No. 2 and bird No. 3 are pictured here.

The WHOOPING CRANE (upper left), America's tallest bird, winters on the coast of Texas and breeds in the neighborhood of Wood Buffalo Park in Canada. Only about two dozen individuals remain in the wild.

The EVERGLADE KITE (lower left) is rapidly losing its last toehold in the marshes around Lake Okeechobee in Florida. It will be a great loss when it goes, but not as great a loss as the Crane, for it also lives outside our country over a range extending from southern Mexico to Argentina.

WHOOPING CRANE

EVERGLADE KITE

96

*Black-billed Cuckoo*

*Yellow-billed Cuckoo*

## CUCKOOS

A friend once remarked that Cuckoos are "clammy birds, hard to get chummy with." But though they have a sinuous, almost reptilian look, and a slow deliberate manner, they are, nevertheless, graceful and good-looking. Cuckoos have thin curved bills and unusual feet with two toes facing to the front and two to the rear. Our kinds with their long tails are longer than Robins but more slender. They are brown above and white below, and because they have no spots on the breast are not likely to be confused, even for a moment, with other brown-backed birds such as Thrushes or Thrashers.

### Yellow-billed Cuckoo

This Cuckoo has a slightly curved *yellowish bill,* bright rusty patches on its wings when it flies, and large white spots in its tail.

### Black-billed Cuckoo

Although both Cuckoos are found well into southern Canada, this is the commonest one in the north. It has a *black bill.* It does not have rusty patches on its wings and only small spots in its tail. Unlike the famous European Cuckoo, our kinds build their own nests.

## THE AUK FAMILY

There are no Penguins in the Arctic. Their realm is the Antarctic. But there is a group of birds that fills their place in the northern oceans. They are shown on the opposite page. Avoiding sandy shores, they nest on rocky islands, from New England, north.

When they fly they look like small Ducks with very stubby necks, but on the rocks seem more like Penguins, standing quite erect, showing white vests and black jackets. Below are the ones the vacationist sees when he visits the sea islands in the Gaspé or elsewhere in the Gulf of St. Lawrence.

### 1. Razor-billed Auk

The heavy head and flat bill marks the Razor-bill. Figure 1a shows the winter plumage.

### 2. Murre

Recognized from the Razor-bill by its thin bill.

### 3. Puffin

Drollest of all seabirds, the chunky Puffin is decorated with a great triangular red bill.

### 4. Black Guillemot

This black seabird has large white wing patches, red feet and a thin bill.

In winter a few stray Auks reach New Jersey, but they are seldom seen away from the ocean. At that season, the black heads become partly white. In addition to those above, the tiny Dovekie (5) might be found. It is the size of a Starling with a very stubby bill. Brunnich's Murre, like a Murre with a shorter bill, sometimes is recorded by experienced bird watchers.

On the Pacific Coast, the Murre is abundant and the Pigeon Guillemot (much like a Black Guillemot) is the next most frequent, but there are many other species not described here.

## OWLS

Owls are all fluff and feathers—perhaps the most shapeless birds—and they look quite neckless. Their big eyes, framed by facial discs, have a slightly more human expression than have the eyes of other birds which are placed more on the sides of their heads. Some Owls are ornamented with "ear tufts" which give them a cat-like look; others are round-headed.

Taking over the night shift when the Hawks have gone to rest, they fly abroad silently and mothlike, until they detect a mouse or some other small creature which they pounce upon with spring-trap claws.

Owls are most easily identified by their heads which are shown on the opposite page. These are the four most familiar kinds:

### Barn Owl

The tawny-colored Barn Owl which hides in old buildings, church belfries and barns is known by its heart-shaped face. It is sometimes called the Monkey-faced Owl. Another buffy Owl is the Short-eared Owl, a streaked day-flying Owl of the marshes. (*See* page 85.)

### Barred Owl

In the wet woodlands and river swamps of the eastern and central states the Barred Owl hoots at night. It has brown eyes, no ears, and is heavily barred across the chest.

### Screech Owl

This small-eared gnome hides during the day in old holes in orchards and shade trees. It might be either bright rusty or gray.

### Great Horned Owl

The big "Cat Owl" has large yellow eyes and a white throat. Another "eared" Owl, the Long-eared Owl (*see* page 85) is Crow-sized with "ears" closer together and a *streaked* belly (Horned Owl, cross-barred).

Barn Owl

Barred Owl

Screech Owl

Great Horned Owl

## GOATSUCKERS

Birds of the night that live a moth-like life. So weak and tiny are their feet and bills as to seem useless, but no moth can escape the cavernous open mouth (surrounded by bristles in Whip-poor-will). The Nighthawk is the most widespread species.

The Nighthawk, in spite of its name, is often seen in the sky, even at noon-day. Its erratic flight, this way and that, and the white patches across its slim wings, identify it.

The Whip-poor-will is a voice in the dark. It seldom flies abroad by day, but nestles unnoticed among the dead leaves. When flushed underfoot, it flits away like a big brown moth, and, if it is a male, flashes white tail patches. Unlike the Nighthawk, its wings are rounded (*See* Dusk Silhouettes, page 153).

## SWIFTS

These sooty Swallow-like birds that look like "flying cigars" twinkle along on narrow bowed wings. Unlike Swallows, they seem to have no tails (they do have a tail of short spiky feathers, however). There is only one kind in the East, the Chimney Swift shown above. In the West, there are three.

## HUMMINGBIRDS

Fantastically like insects, Hummingbirds spend their days among the flowers. They are the smallest birds in the world, with bills like needles and wings like gauze. Most species have iridescent green backs and the males display the colors of every jewel on their throats. Although there are several hundred species in the new-world tropics only one reaches eastern North America, the Ruby-throated Hummingbird (above). The male has a glowing red bib which the female lacks. In the West there are a dozen species. (*See* Western FIELD GUIDE.)

## KINGFISHERS

Of this world-wide family there is only one that ranges widely over our continent. It is the Belted Kingfisher shown here, a big blue-gray bird, longer than a Robin, with a *bushy crest*. Like all Kingfishers it has a big head and a big bill, the better to withstand the headlong dives and to capture minnows. (*See* page 84.)

# WOODPECKERS

Nuthatches, Creepers, and a few other birds climb trees, but not in quite the same way as the Woodpeckers. Climbing upward in short hitches, with its stiff tail braced against the trunk and its head held well back, a Woodpecker climbs a tree with all the professional aplomb of a telephone lineman using spikes and a belt.

Woodpeckers have strong chisel-tipped bills with which they test the diseased wood and dig out the tunnelling grubs. Most species dip up and down when they fly. In fact, this is one of the best ways to tell a Flicker.

Although there are other Woodpeckers, particularly in the West, the five shown here are among the most widespread. All have red somewhere on the head. However, females of the Downy and Hairy Woodpeckers lack the red, but in other ways are like the males.

### Downy Woodpecker

A *white strip* down its back and a small bill identify this small familiar Woodpecker.

### Hairy Woodpecker

Like a large Downy with a *much larger bill*. Both species are found from coast to coast. (*See* page 75.)

### Red-headed Woodpecker

It has the *entire head* red, not just a patch of red as have other Woodpeckers which are often wrongly called "red-heads." It is not found in the West.

### Sapsucker

The *long* white wing-patch marks the Sapsucker and so do the orderly rows of holes it drills.

### Flicker

This *brown* Woodpecker shows a *white rump* as it bounds away. In the East Flickers flash yellow beneath their wings, in the West, red.

Hairy

Downy

Red-headed

Sapsucker

Flicker

## FLYCATCHERS

If you see a small bird sitting quietly in a rather upright pose on a dead branch it is probably a Flycatcher. Should it take off, snap up a flying insect in its small flat bill and return to sit quietly as before, it is almost surely one, although Waxwings and other birds will sometimes act in this manner.

Identification of some of the small Flycatchers is one of the trickiest problems in field ornithology, so I am leaving them for the fuller descriptions in the FIELD GUIDES. Below are the best known species. Learn them before tackling the others.

**Phoebe** (Farms, streams, bridges)

Sparrow-sized, the plain little Phoebe has a gray back, light breast and no outstanding marks (no wing bars, no eye-ring). It constantly *wags its tail.*

**Wood Pewee** (Woods, groves)

Like a Phoebe but with conspicuous light *wing bars.* It does *not* wag its tail.

**Least Flycatcher** (Orchards, groves)

Smaller than a Pewee, it too has wing bars, but unlike the Pewee, also has a conspicuous *eye-ring.* Its "song" is a sharp *che-bek!* In southern woodlands lives the almost identical Acadian Flycatcher. Its sneezy song, *spit-chee!* has a rising inflection. The Least Flycatcher lives mostly in the northern states but the two overlap a bit in New Jersey, Ohio, etc.

**Kingbird** (Roadsides, orchards)

Slightly smaller than a Robin with a dark back, the belligerent Kingbird can be told immediately by the white band across the end of its tail.

**Crested Flycatcher** (Woodlands)

The *rufous tail* is this large Flycatcher's mark. Its belly is pale yellow. (*See* page 74.)

Phoebe

Wood Pewee

Least Flycatcher

Kingbird

Crested Flycatcher

## SWALLOWS

Just as Gulls and Terns are the masters of effortless flight among sea birds, so are Swallows among small land birds. They are Sparrow-sized, but their longer, more pointed wings are cut for speed, maneuverability, and graceful skimming.

Swallows like to sit (rather erectly) in rows on wires, and often several kinds can be recognized among the assemblage. (*See* Roadside Silhouettes, page 157.) The first thing to look for in identifying a Swallow in flight is the color of its back (brown or bluish). Then run it down by the field marks below.

There are only seven common American species, five of which are figured here. These five can be found from coast to coast and from Mexico to Canada.

Swifts are often mistaken for Swallows. (*See* page 102.)

### Purple Martin

Larger than other Swallows, purple-black back
Male: *black breast*
Female: grayish breast

### Barn Swallow

Bluish back; *deeply forked tail*
(It nests on beams usually *inside* barns)

### Cliff Swallow

Bluish back; square tail; *buffy rump* (*See* page 74.)
(It nests under the eaves on the *outside* of barns)

### Tree Swallow

Bluish back; *snow-white breast* (*See* page 74.)
In the West there is another Swallow similar to this species but with white patches that nearly meet on the rump. It is called the Violet-green Swallow.

### Bank Swallow

*Brown* back, band across breast
If you see a brown-backed Swallow that does not have a band across its breast, most likely it is a Rough-winged Swallow.

Barn Swallow

Cliff Swallow

Purple Martin

Bank Swallow

Tree Swallow

*Horned Lark*

*Pipit*

## LARKS

You might not be aware of it, but a Meadowlark is not really a Lark. According to the museum men, it belongs to the Blackbird family. But we do have a true Lark in the United States, a bird with a very long hind claw which shows that it is blood relative to the Skylark of Europe— the Horned Lark, shown above. It is a brown ground bird not much larger than a Sparrow, and it sports black "whiskers" and two tiny black "horns." Wherever there are great expanses of short grass—from coast to coast— it thrives, and on the Great Plains outnumbers all other birds. Perhaps it is the most numerous songbird in the world, for it is found from Mexico to the Arctic Ocean and across the grasslands of Europe and Asia as well, thereby encircling the globe.

## PIPITS

The Pipit represents another old-world family with long hind claws. It comes down from the Arctic barrens to spend the winter on southern fields. So much does it look like a Vesper Sparrow (it is brown with *white outer tail feathers*) that it could be mistaken for it, but it has a thin bill (which shows that it isn't a Sparrow), and it *walks;* and *wags its tail*. Pipits are easily overlooked for some reason, and many more are heard as they fly over than are seen on the ground. (*See* page 73.)

*Blue Jay*

## CROWS and JAYS

The *Corvidae,* which is what ornithologists call this family, are probably the most intelligent birds in the world. Someone has predicted that when man, through his ingenuity, has finally destroyed all his neighbors and himself too, there will still be Crows. No birds are more persecuted than they, yet there are more Crows today than ever. These big black birds have the wits needed to survive. The even larger Ravens of the North also belong to the family and so do the handsome long-tailed Magpies of the West. All are characterized by strong bills, with bristles covering their nostrils.

The Jays are the brightly colored dandies of the family, and of these, the Blue Jay (above), found throughout the East, is the best known. Larger than a Robin, it is the only bright blue bird (east of Rockies) with a *crest.* In the West, there are two widespread Jays, one with a crest —Steller's Jay—that dwells among the pines, and one without a crest—the California or Scrub Jay—that lives in the oaks. (*See* page 80.)

In the section on silhouettes (page 153-64) you will find the silhouettes of Jays, Crows and Magpies. Crows, of course, are so well-known to most people that a description would be superfluous. Some kind of Jay is found in nearly every part of the country but Magpies live only in the West.

*Black=capped Chickadee*　　　*Tufted Titmouse*

## TITMICE

These little acrobats belong to a large old-world family of birds, of which only a dozen species live in the United States. They are smaller than most Sparrows, with slightly longer tails and small stubby bills. Winter woodlands would be dull without them.

### Black-capped Chickadee

A *black cap* and a *black bib* are the trade marks of this little gray bird which lives in the northern and western states; south of Mason and Dixon's Line it is replaced by the Carolina Chickadee, which looks like it, but is smaller. Everyone who feeds birds in winter knows the Chickadees, for they are the first to find the suet. If other birds were marked so clearly and said their names so distinctly we would have no trouble identifying them.

### Tufted Titmouse

This little gray mouse-colored bird is recognized at once by its *crest*. Although it is found as far north as New York City and the Great Lakes, it is most typical of the South. There it is certainly one of the ten commonest birds in the woodlands. In the West, the Plain Titmouse replaces it.

Red-breasted Nuthatch

White-breasted Nuthatch

Brown Creeper

## NUTHATCHES

Nuthatches are chubby little birds, smaller than Sparrows, with strong pick-like bills and stumpy tails. Expert climbers, they need not brace themselves with their tails, nor does it matter whether they go headfirst down the trunk, or up. They are aptly called "upside-down birds." Of the four American species these two are found most widely.

### White-breasted Nuthatch

The black cap and white cheeks mark America's most familiar Nuthatch.

### Red-breasted Nuthatch

A black line through the eye is its mark. It prefers evergreen trees.

## CREEPERS

There is only one species of this family in the New World, the Brown Creeper. It is a slim well-camouflaged little thing, much smaller than a Sparrow, with a thin curved bill and a stiff tail which it uses as a brace. When it climbs a tree it starts at the bottom, hugs the bark and works upwards in spirals.

*House Wren*

*Long-billed Marsh Wren*

## WRENS

Nearly everyone knows "Jenny," the little plump brown bird that cocks its tail over its back. Wrens are smaller and stumpier than Sparrows, with slender bills. Of the 165 species of Wrens in the world (mostly in the American tropics) only nine live in the United States. Two are shown here.

### House Wren

The plainest of the family, a little gray-brown bird with no stripes on its face. It is the best known Wren but not the only one that nests in bird houses. In the southeastern states the big Carolina Wren nests in boxes. It is *rusty,* with a *white stripe* over its eye. (*See* page 90.) In the mid-west and far west lives Bewick's Wren, another box nester, identified by its white eye stripe and *white spots* in the corners of its tail. The smallest and darkest Wren is the Winter Wren (not a box nester). It has a very stubby tail, dark bars on its belly and likes brush piles.

### Long-billed Marsh Wren

Common in the cattails, this lively sprite has *white streaks* on its back, and a white stripe over its eye.

*Golden-crowned Kinglet*

*Ruby-crowned Kinglet*

*Blue-gray Gnatcatcher*

## KINGLETS and GNATCATCHERS

These active midgets belong to the same family of birds as the old-world Warblers, a group that is not at all related to the birds we call Warblers.

### Golden-crowned Kinglet

Kinglets are tiny, short-tailed birds with olive-gray backs and light wing-bars. This species always has a bright patch on its crown; *orange* in males, *yellow* in females.

### Ruby-crowned Kinglet

The Ruby-crown can always be told by its broken eye-ring, but in addition the male has a concealed patch of *ruby-red* on its crown which it will flash if you patiently watch.

### Blue-gray Gnatcatcher

Less than five inches long, this mite looks surprisingly like a tiny Mockingbird. It lives in the South and, like the Mocker, wanders once in a while to New England. Smaller even than a Chickadee, it is blue-gray above, and whitish below, with a white eye-ring and a *long black and white tail* which it flips about.

## THRUSHES

When we think of a Thrush we think of a brown-backed bird with a spotted breast. Actually, the Robin and the Bluebird belong to the family too. We can detect the relationship of these "red-breasted Thrushes" to the "spotted Thrushes" when we see their speckle-breasted young ones.

If we were to describe the features of the family we might say they have large eyes (adapted for seeing in the shadows), moderately slender bills (for poking among the grass and dead leaves) and rather long legs compared to those of other songbirds. Except for the Bluebird, Thrushes spend much of their time on the ground where strong legs are an asset.

Learn the songs from the descriptions in the FIELD GUIDE or from the excellent recording SONGS OF WILD BIRDS (Comstock Publishing Co., Ithaca, N. Y.).

**Robin** (Towns, farms, woodland edges)
  Gray back, *rusty breast*

**Bluebird** (Roadsides, semi-open country)
  Blue back, *rusty breast*

**Wood Thrush** (Eastern deciduous woodlands)
  A spotted Thrush with a *rusty head*

**Hermit Thrush** (Mixed woods of North and West)
  A spotted Thrush with a *rusty tail*

**Veery** (Moist woods, northern states)
  This one is tawny from head to tail, and the spots are not noticeable. In addition to the three brown Thrushes shown here there are two others which show no *rusty* whatsoever. One, the Olive-backed Thrush of the evergreen woods of the North and West has a buffy eye-ring. In the Pacific states a race of this species goes by the name of Russet-backed Thrush. A northern timberline species, the similar Gray-cheeked Thrush has *gray* instead of buffy cheeks.

Robin

Bluebird

Wood Thrush

Hermit Thrush

Veery

## THE MIMIC THRUSHES

These gifted songsters have loose, expressive tails, longer that those of Thrushes, and slender, slightly curved bills. They are larger than most Thrushes (near size of a Robin), and have strong legs, useful for rummaging about on the ground.

### 1. Mockingbird

More slender than a Robin, gray above and white below with *white patches* on its wings and tail

### 2. Catbird

Smaller than a Robin, dark gray all over except the crown which is black, and a patch of *rusty* under the tail.

### 3. Brown Thrasher

A big bright *rusty-red* bird, longer than a Robin. Some people call it "Brown Thrush," but it differs from the Thrushes in having *stripes* instead of spots, light *wing-bars,* a longer tail, and *yellow eyes.* Thrushes have dark eyes.

Cedar Waxwing

Loggerhead Shrike

## WAXWINGS

Dressed in tans and grays, the sleek Waxwings are the most "tailored" birds. They are called Waxwings because of shiny red droplets that look like sealing wax, at the tips of the secondary wing-feathers. But you must be very close to the bird to see this feature. The best field marks are a pointed *crest* and a *yellow band* at the end of the tail. Although there are two Waxwings in North America, only one, the Cedar Waxwing (above) is widespread. The other, the Bohemian Waxwing, flocks mostly to the Rocky Mountain states, where it spends the winter.

## SHRIKES

Shrikes are songbirds with the personality of Hawks. Even their beaks have hooked tips, and they wear a bandit's mask. Otherwise they look something like Mockingbirds, gray with black wings and tail. Perched on a wire or a tree-top they wait until they spot a grasshopper or a mouse. Sometimes a small bird is taken. The habit of impaling their prey on thorns gives them the nickname "Butcher Birds." Only two of the world's seventy-seven Shrikes live here. One, the Loggerhead Shrike (above), is widespread throughout the United States. (*See* page 90.) The other, the Northern Shrike, visits the northern states only in winter.

## VIREOS

"Vireo," broadly translated, means *I am green*. This is a good name for these little olive-backed (or gray-olive) birds. Most kinds have whitish breasts, often with a tinge of yellowish on the sides. The size of small Sparrows, they look at first glance much like their tree-top competitors, the Warblers. But Vireos are slower in their movements, and their bills (bottom of page) are a little thicker, with a more curved ridge. In identifying a Vireo, see first whether it has *wing-bars* or lacks them; then run it down by its "field marks," below. The four most widely-known species are shown here. The Red-eyed Vireo is perhaps the most numerous bird east of the Mississippi.

**Red-eyed Vireo** (Woodlands)
  No wing-bars; gray crown
  Conspicuous black and white eyebrow stripes

**Warbling Vireo** (Shade trees, groves)
  No wing-bars; less conspicuous light eyebrow line

**Blue-headed Vireo** (Mixed evergreen woodlands)
  Wing-bars, white throat; white eye-ring. Its white eye
    ring causes some people to think it is a White-eyed
    Vireo, a more southern species.

**Yellow-throated Vireo** (Deciduous woodlands)
  Wing-bars, *bright yellow throat* and breast

*Vireo*

*Warbler*

Red-eyed Vireo

Warbling Vireo

Blue=headed Vireo

Yellow-throated Vireo

*Yellow
Warbler*

*Redstart*

## WARBLERS

The Wood Warblers, strictly an American family, are the gay butterflies among birds. In most woodlands in the United States, one bird in six is a Warbler of some kind, while in many of the Canadian forests, half of the birds present in summer are Warblers. In late spring, when they migrate through in great waves, they are a delight to identify.

Although fifty-four species cross our borders, only the males of twenty are shown in these pages. The FIELD GUIDES cover them all, showing both sexes in color. Most Warblers run to yellows and are smaller than Sparrows (except the Chat), with small thin bills, designed for picking up tiny insects. Some Warblers act like Flycatchers at times.

The Redstart (above) is probably the most numerous Warbler in the woodlands of the East. Males with their orange wing and tail patches and females with similar yellow patches cannot be mistaken.

The best known species is the Yellow Warbler which looks *all yellow* at any distance. Males have reddish streaks on the breast and *yellow spots* in the tail, a feature shared only by the female Redstart. (*See* page 82.)

## WARBLERS *Without* WING-BARS

Before you get down to the field-marks, the thing to notice first when you see a Warbler is—*does it have wing-bars?* If it has *not,* such as the ones whose heads are shown on this page, usually it also *lacks streaks* (the Canada Warbler is an exception). Most of these live close to the ground. Only males are shown.

1. **Yellow-Throat** (Wet open spots; clearings)
   Black *mask,* yellow throat

2. **Hooded Warbler** (Undergrowth in dense woods)
   Black *hood,* yellow cheeks

3. **Wilson's Warbler** (Brushy thickets)
   Black *cap,* yellow underparts

4. **Prothonotary Warbler** (Swamps; mostly south)
   Golden-orange head, blue-gray wings

5. **Canada Warbler** (Moist rocky woodlands)
   "Necklace" of streaks, yellow "spectacles"

## WARBLERS *With* WING-BARS

When a Warbler has wing-bars, as do the ones whose heads are shown opposite, it usually has *streaks* too (exceptions are the Parula Warbler which has wing-bars but no streaks, and the Black-throated Blue Warbler which has a small patch of white in the wing instead of bars). Most of these are tree-loving Warblers. Only males are shown.

1. **Black and White Warbler** (Tree trunks, limbs)
   Black and white stripes

2. **Blackpoll Warbler** (Tree tops)
   Black cap, white cheeks

3. **Blackburnian Warbler** (Evergreen trees)
   Fire-orange throat

4. **Chestnut-sided Warbler** (Bushes, slashings)
   Chestnut sides, yellow cap (*see* page 82)

5. **Myrtle Warbler** (All trees, shrubs)
   Yellow crown, yellow rump. In the West, a similar
   bird is Audubon's Warbler

6. **Magnolia Warbler** (Small evergreens in summer)
   Black back, heavily striped yellow breast, white band
   across center of tail

7. **Black-throated Blue Warbler** (Woodlands)
   Black throat, blue-gray back

8. **Black-throated Green Warbler** (Evergreen trees)
   Black throat, yellow cheeks (*see* page 82)

9. **Parula Warbler** (Spanish moss or Usnea)
   Bluish above, yellow below, breast band

10. **Prairie Warbler** (Pine barrens, scrub oak)
    Two face stripes; wags its tail. Another tail wagger,
    the Palm Warbler, has a rusty cap (*see* page 82)

Ovenbird     Water-thrush     Chat

## OTHER WARBLERS

There are several members of the family that do not go by the name of Warbler. In fact, the following three do not seem like Warblers at all.

**Ovenbird** (Woodlands)

Like a small Thrush, the Ovenbird is big-eyed with spots on its breast. It even *walks* in the manner of a Thrush. Its *dull orange crown* identifies it.

**Water-thrush** (Streams, swamps)

Water-thrushes, on the other hand, seem more like little Shorebirds. They teeter their tails as vigorously as Spotted Sandpipers. The stripe over the eye and the striped underparts are their marks. There are two kinds, the Louisiana and the Northern Water-thrush.

**Chat** (Bushes, tangles)

Perhaps environment molds the character of birds. The Chat not only has the loose-tailed look of the Mockers and Catbirds with which it shares the bushes and briers, but it sings a similar song. Its large size (7½ inches), yellow breast and white "spectacles" identify it.

## THE BLACKBIRD FAMILY

Our Orioles are not Orioles, nor is the Meadowlark a Lark. The true Orioles and Larks are old-world families. Our Orioles and Meadowlarks, believe it or not, belong to the Blackbird family. And to make it all the more confusing, the bird they call a "Blackbird" in Europe is really a Thrush!

It is difficult to describe the Blackbirds as a group except that they have conical, sharp pointed bills and rather flat foreheads.

**Bobolink** (Fields, meadows) (*See* page 73.)
This is the only songbird that is *black below* and *white above*. Females are buffy-brown with striped heads.

**Meadowlark** (Fields, meadows)
Chunky, brown, with *white outer tail feathers*, and a black V on a yellow breast.

**Baltimore Oriole** (Shade trees, especially elms)
*Fiery orange* with a black head and back. Females are duller; yellow-orange with wing-bars. In the South and West, five other Orioles are found.

# BLACKBIRDS

When Blackbirds fly over in big flocks, *notice the length of their tails*. If their tails are *long* they are Grackles. If they are *short* they are Starlings. If they are of medium length they are Red-wings, Cowbirds, or one of the other Blackbirds. Study the Sky Silhouettes on page 165.

### Red-wing

Bright *red shoulders* or "epaulettes" make this Blackbird of the marshes and swamps unmistakable. Females are dusky brown, with heavy stripes on the breast. In western marshes Red-wings enjoy the company of Yellow-headed Blackbirds.

### Grackle

This is the glossy *long-tailed* Blackbird that walks on the lawns. The tail is often creased down the center, creating a keel-like effect. The very large Grackles one sees along tidewater on the South Atlantic coast are Boat-tailed Grackles. There are no Grackles west of the Rockies, but there is a bird everywhere that looks like one, except that its tail is shorter. It is Brewer's Blackbird. Another similar species is the Rusty Blackbird that migrates through eastern river swamps to its summer home in Canada.

### Cowbird

The smallest Blackbird has a *brown head* and a short Sparrow-like bill. Females are gray.

### Starling

This immigrant from Europe is not a true Blackbird, but belongs to an old-world family. It is placed here because we automatically compare it with the Blackbirds. It has a *short tail,* and in spring, a *yellow bill.* At close range it is glossed with purple and green, and sprinkled with tiny light spots. In winter the bill is dark and the spots more noticeable

Red-wing

Cowbird

Grackle

Starling

_Scarlet Tanager_

## TANAGERS

Matching orchids in brilliance, Tanagers make the tropics gay. Although there are four hundred species only four reach the United States. They suggest that other tropical family of infinite variety, the Hummingbirds, of which only one species, the Ruby-throat, flies to eastern Canada. Another adventurous species, the Rufous Hummer, ranges to western Canada. In like manner, the Scarlet Tanager, shown above, is the eastern offshoot of the Tanager tribe. _Vivid scarlet_ with _black wings_ (see page 83), it prefers the larger trees, especially oaks. Its western counterpart, the Western Tanager (the West's most showy bird) has a _crimson head,_ yellow breast and black back. Throughout the southern states, the Summer Tanager is found. Also a lover of oaks (especially live oaks) , it is _all red_ without the black wings of the Scarlet Tanager. Male Tanagers are the brilliant sex. Females are greenish with yellowish breasts. (See page 94.)

Ornithologists are not certain where to draw the dividing line between Tanagers and Finches because they are so much alike in some ways. A Tanager's bill is rather thick, longer than a Sparrow's, with a notch on its cutting edge. (See inset.)

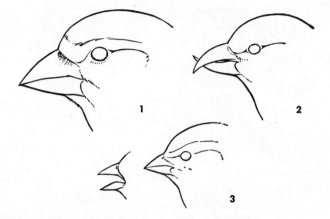

## THE FINCH AND SPARROW FAMILY

This is the largest family of birds in the world (over 1200 species and subspecies). Authorities put them at the very peak of the birds' "family tree." The one feature which they share in common is their bills, which are *short and thick* with a sharp cutting angle at the base for cracking seeds. These, however, take several shapes (above) — (1) very stout (Grosbeaks); (2) crossed like pruning shears (Crossbills); or (3) somewhat like the bill of a Canary (Sparrows, Buntings, etc.).

The House Sparrow or English Sparrow (male below), familiar to everyone, is not a true Finch, but belongs to a separate old-world family called WEAVER FINCHES.

*House Sparrow*

## FINCHES, ETC.

1. **Rose-breasted Grosbeak** (Young tree growth)
   *Rose-red triangle* on breast. The female is like a large streaked Sparrow with a big bill.

2. **Cardinal** (Thickets, gardens)
   All red, the only *red* bird with a *crest*. Females are tan with red tails, red bills. (*See* page 90.)

3. **Indigo Bunting** (Roadsides, bushes, slashings)
   *Deep blue all over.* Females are tan with no distinctive marks. (*See* page 83.)

4. **Goldfinch** (Roadsides, orchards, gardens)
   *Bright yellow* with *black wings.* Females are olive.

5. **Purple Finch** (Small evergreens; other trees)
   Rosy-red (like a Sparrow dipped in wine) . The female is like a heavily streaked Sparrow.

6. **Junco** (Roadsides, fields, edges)
   Slate gray with *white outer tail feathers.*

7. **Snow Bunting** (Fields and shores in winter)
   Big *white patches* in the wings.

8. **Towhee** (Brushy places)
   *Rusty sides,* big white tail-spots. It rummages about on the ground and in thickets.

9. **Red Crossbill** (Evergreens) , Head, page 131
   Deep *brick red* with a *cross-tipped bill.* Females are dull olive yellow with dark wings.

## SPARROWS (With *Unstreaked* Breasts)

In contrast to the gaudier members of the Finch family, the Sparrows are plain, streaked with brown. To identify them, see first *whether the breast is streaked* or not. Then go on from there. Those whose heads are shown on the page opposite are *without* streaks. They in turn fall into two groups.

### A. SPARROWS WITH *Striped* CAPS

**White-throated Sparrow** (Brushy places)

White head stripes and a *white throat* identify it. It likes to scratch about among the dead leaves.

**White-crowned Sparrow** (Brushy places)

If it has white head stripes but a *grayish throat* it is this species. Its bill is *pink*. White-throated Sparrows are mainly eastern birds; the White-crown becomes much more numerous as you go westward. (*See* page 83.)

### B. SPARROWS WITH *Rusty* CAPS

**Chipping Sparrow** (Orchards, gardens, farms)

The "Chippy" is the tame little red-capped Sparrow with the white stripe over its eye.

**Tree Sparrow** (Fields, roadsides, marshes)

This is the "Winter Chippy" that comes down from northern Canada when the snow flies. It has a *single black spot* on its plain breast.

**Field Sparrow** (Pastures, small bushes)

A *pink bill* is its trade mark. Although it is named Field Sparrow you will not find it in the open meadows. It must have bushes.

**Swamp Sparrow** (Fresh marshes, swamps)

This rusty-capped Sparrow that lurks among the cattails shows a gray breast and a white throat.

*White-throated*

*White-crowned*

*Chipping*

*Tree*

*Field*

*Swamp*

## SPARROWS (With *Streaked* Breasts)

Besides these three streak-breasted Sparrows which are basic for every beginner to know, there are several other more obscure kinds (like the wide-spread Savannah Sparrow) that live in the meadows, prairies, and salt marshes. *See* page 218, FIELD GUIDE TO THE BIRDS.

**Song Sparrow** (Hedgerows, gardens, roadsides)

The best-known native Sparrow. The streaks gather into a *heavy spot* in the center of the breast.

**Vesper Sparrow** (Open grassy fields)

When it flies look for *white outer tail feathers.*

**Fox Sparrow** (Brushy places, thickets)

This heavily-striped bird, the largest Sparrow, scratches busily among the leaves. Look for a *rusty tail* when it flies. It is the first bird to migrate northward to Canada in early spring.

*Song Sparrow*

*Vesper Sparrow*

*Fox Sparrow*

# IV

## HABITATS

## (Where to Look for Birds)

## THE TOWNS AND FARMS

Although I have seen thousands of Meadowlarks, perhaps tens of thousands, I have never found one in a woods. And I have never seen a Wood Thrush in a meadow. Just as a fisherman lives near the sea, a lumberjack in the forest and a cab driver in the city, so each bird has its niche—its place in the sun. The bird watcher knows this and when he goes out in the morning to run up a list he does not remain in one kind of place. He does not stay all day in the woods. After a bit, he investigates a meadow, or explores a pond or a swamp. The more birds he finds the more fun it is.

A few birds do invade environments other than their own at times, especially in migration. A Warbler that spends the summer in Maine might be seen, on its journey through Florida, in a palm tree. In cities, migrating birds have to make the best of it, like the Woodcock found one morning on a window ledge of the General Motors Building in New York City outside the former office of the National Audubon Society.

A few birds are well adapted to the steel and concrete of the big cities—birds like the Starling, English Sparrow and Pigeon. Chimney Swifts, Nighthawks and Martins skim the sky over the downtown business section and even nest on some of the buildings. So do a few Kestrels (Sparrow Hawks) and recently even the Peregrine, the wildest of the Hawks, has nested on the high buildings of five or six American cities.

Where the sterile core of the city gives way to houses with lawns and gardens there are Robins, House Wrens, Chipping Sparrows, Song Sparrows, Yellow Warblers, and Grackles. Where shade trees are large, Warbling Vireos and Baltimore Orioles swing their nests. In more southern cities Cardinals, Mockingbirds and Carolina Wrens dwell in every garden.

It is hard to draw the line between the birds of the farm and those of the town because rural conditions blend at the city's edge. Farm buildings have their bird tenants; Phoebes and Barn Swallows nest on the rafters, and Cliff Swallows under the eaves. There might even be a pair of Barn Owls. Cowbirds invade the cattle yard, and Pheasants sometimes pilfer the scratchfeed, but this elegant fowl, and its little brother, the Bob-white, usually stick close to the brushy fencerows, using them as "streets" by which they travel from meadow to meadow. Catbirds and Thrashers skulk in these thickets too and dart across the road. The birds of the roadside, like Kingbirds, Shrikes, Song Sparrows and Bluebirds are essentially farm country birds. (*See* Roadside Silhouettes, page 157.)

Bluebirds readily accept bird houses and so do Tree Swallows and a dozen other species. The Purple Martin, as a matter of fact, is completely won over to boxes, but most of the others still prefer an old knot hole in the orchard. Orchards always have a high density of birds, not only of hole nesters like Wrens, Titmice, Wood-peckers, Crested Flycatchers and Screech Owls, but also Robins, Wood Pewees, Least Flycatchers, Waxwings, Goldfinches and a number of others. Abandoned orchards, of course, are much better than sprayed ones.

## FIELDS AND MEADOWS

When man, the great disturber, swings his axe and clears a farm, he does not wipe out bird life. He merely swaps Woodpeckers for Meadowlarks.

In his hayfields, in addition to Meadowlarks, there might be Bobolinks, or Grasshopper and Vesper Sparrows —perhaps even Upland Plovers, whistling eerily on the wind. On the more northern farms, Savannah Sparrows invade the fields, while in the midwest, Dickcissels revel in the alfalfa. Where cattle have chewed the grass so short that bald patches of hard earth are exposed, Horned Larks take possession. These Larks also like golf courses, and so does the Killdeer. Both nest early and often take advantage of plowed fields before the green growth covers the furrows.

Many birds that do not nest there use the meadows as a happy hunting ground. Swallows skim close to the waving grass and climb upwards into the blue. In late summer and fall, Mourning Doves, Crows and great flocks of Blackbirds search the stubble, while Sparrow Hawks, Marsh Hawks and Red-tails quarter back and forth in their never-ending quest for meadow mice. When frosts touch the dark turf with silver, Pipits pass by on their trek from the Arctic tundra to the southern states. Later, transient Tree Sparrows foretell the snows. Some remain all winter with the flocks of Snow Buntings that glean the seeds from the brown weeds that protrude through the bleak drifts.

## BRUSHY PLACES

When a field goes fallow, permitting the weeds and small bushes to take over, Song Sparrows and Field Sparrows become interested. Pheasants and Bob-whites now find it safer to leave the hedgerows than it was when the grass was an unbroken carpet of green.

If this is allowed to go on, nature will attempt to reclaim the meadow; to return it to the forest. The bushes increase in height from four feet to eight, then ten. They soon become spindly saplings. In less than a century these second-growth trees mature and where once grass had been, there is again a grand old forest. During the time the plants are changing the birds change too. We call this process "succession."

This process goes on even more rapidly when a wood has been cut and then allowed to reforest itself. There are almost always Field Sparrows, Towhees, Catbirds, and Thrashers in the slashings. In the southern and central states, White-eyed Vireos and Chats sing loudly from the brier tangles, while in the northern tier of states Chestnut-sided Warblers are numerous. Cuckoos, Goldfinches, and a number of other species also find the young growth to their liking. One of the most abundant birds of all in some sections is the Indigo Bunting. In the Appalachian hills this gorgeous blue Finch inhabits every burn and slashing where the bushes are not over six or eight feet high. As the growth becomes taller these birds drop out and others replace them.

## DECIDUOUS WOODLANDS

When the first anchor chains rattled off American
shores, the primeval forest was far different from most
woodlands today. Many of the trees were much larger,
and they were spaced more openly, with smaller trees
and shrubs in between. There was a healthy balance
of young and old trees, and, in spots, the sunlight even
reached the ground. Fine woodlands can be compared
to cities in which trees are the inhabitants—young folks,
old folks, some being born, some growing up, others
dying.

Foresters, at least the more thoughtful ones, now believe it is better to crop trees selectively, taking some
here and some there, rather than to level the forest at
a sweep. For trees cannot be regimented any more than
men. Consider a second-growth woodlot in which all the
trees are about thirty years old. They are crowded, and
little light reaches the forest floor. There might be Red-
eyed Vireos in the green canopy above, or Ovenbirds
in the shade below—but little else. And because bird life
is scant, an insect scourge might, at any year, sweep
through, killing many of the trees. Or there might be a
dry year when there is not enough moisture for all
the trees, so some die. It is nature's way of opening up the
forest, of giving new growth a chance, and of creating
variety.

You can see then, why the edge has more birds than
the heart of the woods. It is the point of transition, where

competition among plants is keenest. There is everything from grass to grown trees. Ornithologists have coined the term "edge" to describe all borderline environments, whether it be an open spot in the woods, the edge of the woods, or the edge of a swamp, meadow or roadside. In such places bird watchers always have their best luck.

Some birds, like Redstarts and Rose-breasted Grosbeaks, prefer the younger trees. Tanagers and Wood Pewees like the larger trees, especially the oaks. Woodpeckers can't live in a woods until it has aged a bit; not until there is some dead timber. In their wake follow other hole nesters—Crested Flycatchers, Chickadees, Titmice, and White-breasted Nuthatches—species that live in natural cavities, or in holes that the Woodpeckers have abandoned.

There is a difference in the bird life of the upland woods and that of the bottomland. Grouse, Whip-poorwills, and Broad-winged Hawks live in the drier woods, where Ovenbirds chant from the leafy floor and Hooded Warblers sing in the laurel thickets (the Hooded, however, might also be found in some swamps). Red-eyed Vireos, Yellow-throated Vireos, Wood Thrushes, Black and White Warblers, Tanagers and most of the hole nesters are impartial to either type of habitat. But Veeries, Barred Owls, and Red-shouldered Hawks prefer the low creek bottoms, and, in more southern sections, so do Gnatcatchers, Acadian Flycatchers, Caroline Wrens, and Kentucky Warblers. In the Mississippi Valley, in addition to these, Cerulean Warblers range through the leafy trees.

Of all those mentioned above, the three most numerous woodland birds in eastern North America are perhaps the Red-eyed Vireo, Redstart and Ovenbird.

To be complete in our list of woodland species we should include the birds of the "edges," birds like Robins, Towhees, and a host of others, but they are catalogued more properly in the sections on farms and brushy places. They seldom penetrate the thick woods, for they are lovers of sunlight.

## EVERGREEN WOODLANDS

In the cool forests of hemlock and spruce where Winter Wrens sing, at least half of the birds during the summer months are Warblers. These coniferous forests span Canada, cross the northern border of the United States and follow the crests of the higher mountains into the southern states.

Flickers, and Downy and Hairy Woodpeckers thrive in any kind of a woods, for to them, dead wood is dead wood. Blue-headed Vireos and Hermit Thrushes like mixed woodlands, but Olive-backed Thrushes prefer pure stands of evergreens. Chickadees are indifferent to the kind of forest it is, but Red-breasted Nuthatches and Kinglets are obligated to the conifers. At the edges of the open spots where blueberries invade the moss, Juncos, White-throated Sparrows, and Purple Finches sing from the small firs.

But the real show is put on by the Warblers—Nashville Warblers at the edges of the bogs, Chestnutsides in the slashings, Magnolias and Myrtles in the smaller evergreens, Parulas where usnea moss drapes the limbs, and Black-throated Greens and Blackburnians among the taller trees. North of the Canadian boundary, Cape May and Bay-breasted Warblers become more frequent, and so do Blackpoll and Palm Warblers. Besides all these, there are Crossbills, Siskins, Canada Jays, Lincoln Sparrows, Yellow-bellied and Olive-sided Flycatchers, and, where the trees become more stunted, Wilson's Warblers, Fox Sparrows, and Gray-cheeked Thrushes.

## PINE BARRENS

Pines are evergreens, but we do not think of the sandy barrens of pine and scrub oak, especially those near the coast from Cape Cod to Florida, in the same way that we do the cool hemlock and fir forests of the North. The bird life is quite different. In fact, most coastal pine barren country makes rather dull birding (inland pine barrens such as those in northern Michigan often have more variety).

Flickers and Downy and Hairy Woodpeckers like the barrens at any time of year, and so do Chickadees, Blue Jays and Crows. Red-tailed Hawks hunt there by day, and Great Horned Owls take over the night shift when the Whip-poor-wills start to call. Pine Warblers trill like Chippies from the taller pines (there are Chipping Sparrows there too), and Prairie Warblers sing their wiry notes "like a mouse with a tooth-ache" from the oak scrub. Other birds that share the hot scrubby thickets are Catbirds, Brown Thrashers, Towhees, Field Sparrows and Yellow-throats. On Long Island and Cape Cod a few Hermit Thrushes live among the pitch pines. Farther south in the barrens, from Virginia and the Carolinas to Florida, Brown-headed Nuthatches, Yellow-throated Warblers (*see* page 90), Red-cockaded Woodpeckers, and Pinewoods Sparrows can be found. A few other species, but not many, invade the barrens in migration and in winter.

Pine barren country is so often swept by fire that much of it stays scrubby, and the trees do not reach the size of those above.

## FRESH MARSHES

Wet feet are the price you pay if you would be a bog-trotter. But your bird list will soar, for few environments have a higher density of birds than a swamp or a marsh —nine or ten birds per acre, on an average, and often far more than that, particularly in migration. A marsh is a half-way point in succession—land being created where once there had been water.

Start your day in a cattail marsh and revel in the dawn chorus. When the frog voices subside, Rails whinny and grunt; Coots, Gallinules and Pied-billed Grebes call loudly, American Bitterns pump, and Least Bitterns coo. Long-billed Marsh Wrens bubble from the reeds all over the marsh and Short-billed Marsh Wrens chatter in the grassy sedge. Red-wings, displaying their epaulettes, gurgle *o-ka-leeee,* and Swamp Sparrows trill like musical Chippies. Besides all these, there might be Swallows of two or three species skimming overhead, Yellow-throats, a few Marsh Ducks, Herons wading about, and perhaps a Marsh Hawk or two.

Southern marshes have the most Herons, mid-western and far-western marshes the most nesting Ducks. During the flood-tide of migration, hosts of Waterfowl, Snipe, Shorebirds, Swallows, Bobolinks, Grackles and other Blackbirds swarm through the marshes that follow the drainage pattern of the continent. Marshes should be preserved not only for wildlife but also to stabilize our country's water-table.

## FRESH PONDS and CREEKS

These may be of two or three kinds, those in the marshes or in open country and those surrounded by trees. A pond in the marsh would be populated by most of the birds mentioned on the previous page, but they are easier to see. Swallows skim the mirror-like water, Pied-billed Grebes float in full view, and, in season, Marsh Ducks (Blacks, Mallards, Pintails, Teal, Bald-pates, Shovellers, etc.) dabble in the pondweed. Herons wade the shallows and even Rails, so difficult to find when they are hidden among the reeds, sometimes venture to the water's edge.

Wooded ponds have a different flavor. Green Herons resort to them more than do other Herons, and Wood Ducks, Ring-necked Ducks and Hooded Mergansers are at home there. (To the north, such ponds harbor Loons.) Spotted Sandpipers run up and down the narrow strip of shore, and, in migration, so do Solitary Sandpipers. The latter two waders also explore the wooded creeks where Water-thrushes teeter along the margin. Here Kingfishers rattle around the bends; Phoebes nest under the small bridges and Yellow Warblers dart from the willows. In the more southern states Prothonotary Warblers flash like golden flames against the dark water. Song Sparrows, Swamp Sparrows, Yellow-throats, Catbirds and Woodcock populate the swamp thickets, and a host of others intrude, including all the typical birds of the bottomland woods, described on page 142.

## LAKES and BAYS

During migration the lakes are at their best. In states like Pennsylvania and West Virginia, where natural lakes are rare, artificial lakes and reservoirs are a paradise for tired Ducks travelling overland. If there are marshes in the coves, the usual surface-feeding Marsh Ducks stop. But in deeper water Diving Ducks assemble in rafts. It is exciting to sweep the water from right to left with a glass and pick up Scaup, Canvasbacks, Redheads, Golden-eyes, Buffleheads, Mergansers, Ruddy Ducks and other divers such as Coots, Loons, and Horned Grebes. Gulls often resort to inland lakes, especially Herring, Ring-billed and Bonaparte's Gulls, and so do Terns—Common and Black Terns mostly, but Caspian Terns are frequent on the Great Lakes. Ospreys, Bald Eagles, and Kingfishers cruise over the water, looking for fish, while Herons stand motionless at the edge. Swallows actually compete with the fish by deftly snatching up floating insects.

The salt bays and estuaries, protected from the sea by the long barrier beaches, also have a bird roster like that above. In addition, there are Laughing Gulls, Black Skimmers, and Least Terns. Cormorants and Sea Ducks, such as Scoters and Old-squaws, often seek respite in these sheltered waters. Brant, Canada Geese and Black Ducks congregate there and Swans make certain estuaries be-tween Maryland and North Carolina their winter head-quarters. They are the same Swans that stop on the Great Lakes on the way to the Arctic.

## SALT MARSHES

From the elbow of Cape Cod to Key West, and west-ward along the Gulf of Mexico, the sand beaches stretch endlessly. Behind these barrier islands lie vast salt marshes, protected from the sea. Here tidal channels— the "inland waterway"—afford both men and birds a highway down the coast.

Clapper Rails clatter from the channel's edge, and Seaside and Sharp-tailed Sparrows gasp their weak songs These three are the most exclusive residents of the salt marsh. You will not find them elsewhere. Laughing Gulls are strictly salt marsh nesters too, but they wander more widely.

Red-wings, Long-billed Marsh Wrens and Meadow-larks nest where their ecological requirements are met, and, in the thickets at the edge of the marsh, the birds listed on the next page reside.

Herons and Egrets invade the salt meadows in summer and so do migrating shorebirds which feed on the mud flats at low tide and rest in a dry part of the marsh when the water is high. In the south, Forster's Terns and Boat tailed Grackles are a familiar sight.

Bobolinks, Savannah Sparrows, Tree Swallows and Barn Swallows are abundant in migration, and winter finds Black Ducks more numerous than they were in summer. At this season, Sparrow Hawks, Marsh Hawks, Rough-legged Hawks (see page 86), and Short-eared Owls hunt the mice that throng the meadows.

## SAND DUNES and COASTAL THICKETS

The sand dunes with their sparse covering of beach grass stand as a bulwark between the ocean winds and the marshes to the lee. There bird life is scant except for Savannah and Ipswich Sparrows in migration and, in winter, wintering flocks of Horned Larks and Snow Buntings, and stray Snowy Owls (*see* page 89), Piping Plovers and Spotted Sandpipers sometimes nest on the level stretches, but they prefer the beach shelf where the Terns raise their families.

But in the dense scrubby thickets of bayberries, poison ivy and high-tide bush that lie tucked in the hollows between the dunes and the salt marsh, birds are plentiful. In summer there are Brown Thrashers, Catbirds, Towhees, Yellow Warblers, Yellow-throats, Red-wings, and Song Sparrows. In some patches of stunted trees a few Green Herons and Black-crowned Night Herons can always be found. Dune thickets on the shores of the Great Lakes are similar.

During migration almost any bird off the beaten path might turn up. These thickets are to birds what an oasis in the desert is to men. Kingbirds, Swallows, Thrushes, Kinglets, Red-eyed Vireos and eight or ten kinds of Warblers are especially frequent. Myrtle Warblers and Flickers remain all winter because of the bayberries, and, farther south, so do Tree Swallows. At this season, Song Sparrows, White-throats, Fox Sparrows, Tree Sparrows and Juncos also populate the tangles.

## BEACHES and MUD FLATS

The long sand beaches are the meeting place of land and sea, and the birds that live along this point of contact are the greatest travellers on earth. In summer there are Piping Plovers, Spotted Sandpipers, Common and Least Terns, and Skimmers. The Sanderling is the most typical bird of the outer beaches. Little parties can be seen whisking back and forth nearly every month of the year. During migration other shorebirds join them—Turnstones, Black-bellied Plovers, Knots, and Semipalmated and Red-backed Sandpipers. There are many Gulls too, especially in winter, at which season the Horned Larks and Snow Buntings glean the tide-drift.

But if you wish to see birds by the hundreds, *head for the inlets,* where the sea breaks through. There, on the tip point, rest Gulls and Terns, while on the mud flats behind, Herons and shorebirds feed. Watch the tide tables, and remember that no habitat can boast more birds per square yard than a good mud flat at low tide. In migration, Semipalmated and Least Sandpipers, Yellowlegs, Dowitchers, Curlew and a host of others swarm the flats. In winter there is less to see, but there are always many Black Ducks and Gulls.

Beaches and flats on inland lakes are similar, especially on the Great Lakes and on prairie lakes. Even muddy fields, golf courses and airports attract many shorebirds at times. Golf courses near the coast are especially good during northeast storms in fall.

## THE OCEAN

In summer, scantily-clad bathers monopolize the surf, but if you go offshore in a fishing boat you stand a chance of finding something besides the ever-present Gulls and Terns. If you go out far enough you are almost sure to see Wilson's Petrels, like Swallow-like black birds with white rumps. They like to flit in the wake of boats. You might see Shearwaters, scaling on stiff wings close to the waves, or Phalaropes (like small swimming Sandpipers), or even a Jaeger, chasing the Terns. These are the birds the average bird watcher knows the least. Rarely are they seen from land, but patient watching from the dunes is sometimes rewarded by a glimpse of one.

The sea is at its best in winter, and the most favorable vantage point is some headland like Montauk Point, or an inlet. Loons and Grebes dive beyond the surf, and in certain places rafts of Sea Ducks gather—American, Surf and White-winged Scoters—and smaller groups of Red-breasted Mergansers and Old-squaws. In a few places in New England Eiders congregate. There are far more Gulls in winter (including Black-backs and Kittiwakes, the latter usually far offshore), but the Terns have gone from the more northern waters. The prize find is one of the Auk family: a Razor-bill, Murre, Puffin or Dovekie. The Gannets that drop like white rockets into the water, and the Cormorants are more numerous during migration.

## THE WEST

This little book is slanted toward the East. From an ornithological point of view, the birds are much the same from the Atlantic to the Mississippi and beyond—to about the 100th degree of longitude on the high plains. There, one eastern bird after another drops out, and western species replace them. Even so, nearly half the birds of the United States can be found both in the East and the West. The Ducks are almost identical, and the majority of shorebirds, Terns and Hawks are the same. Songbirds differ more widely, but even many of them are transcontinental.

The high mountains make it possible to have a wet, dry, hot or cold climate within a few hours reach, and, in the southwest particularly, to duplicate landscapes like those of the Mexican desert and those of northern Canada. You will notice, when you ascend the mountains, that the plants change as you climb. The brown grass of the valleys gives way to oaks, then pines take over, and finally firs prevail before timber-line is reached. With each change in vegetation there is a change in the bird life. To find such variety in the East you would have to travel from Florida to the Gulf of St. Lawrence or Newfoundland.

There are, in all, more species between the Rockies and the Pacific than there are in the eastern and central states. For a full account of them and their portraits, consult A FIELD GUIDE TO WESTERN BIRDS.

# V

## SILHOUETTES
## OF COMMON BIRDS

## DUSK SILHOUETTES

1. Bat (not a bird)
2. Nighthawk
3. Whip-poor-will
4. Night Heron
5. Screech Owl
6. Woodcock

# ROADSIDE SILHOUETTES

1. Kingfisher
2. Song Sparrow
3. House Sparrow
4. Purple Martin
5. Barn Swallow
6. Tree Swallow
7. Cliff Swallow
8. Bluebird

9. Grackle
10. Red-wing
11. Starling
12. Cowbird
13. Hummingbird
14. Kingbird
15. Robin
16. Shrike

# ROADSIDE SILHOUETTES

1. Mockingbird
2. Cuckoo
3. Cardinal
4. Blue Jay
5. Cedar Waxwing
6. Horned Lark
7. Upland Plover
8. Phoebe
9. Pheasant
10. Mourning Dove
11. Flicker
12. Meadowlark
13. Bob-white
14. Killdeer
15. Crow

# ROADSIDE SILHOUETTES

## (Typical mostly of the West and Southwest)

1. Sparrow Hawk
2. Red-tailed Hawk
3. Turkey Vulture
4. Burrowing Owl
5. Steller's Jay (Pines)
6. California or Scrub Jay
   (Oaks)

7. Nighthawk
8. Scissor-tailed Flycatcher
9. Magpie
10. California Quail
11. Road-runner

# SHORE SILHOUETTES

1. Great Blue Heron
2. Night Heron
3. Green Heron
4. Clapper Rail
5. Marbled Godwit
6. Dowitcher
7. Hudsonian Curlew
8. Yellow-legs
9. Black Skimmer
10. Herring Gull

11. Common Tern
12. Semipalmated Sandpiper
13. Sanderling
14. Spotted Sandpiper
15. Black-bellied Plover
16. Ringed (Semipalmated) Plover
17. Ruddy Turnstone
18. Killdeer

# WATER SILHOUETTES

1. Cormorant
2. Loon
3. Herring Gull
4. Black Skimmer
5. Phalarope (Northern)
6. Merganser (Red-breasted)
7. Coot

8. Common Tern
9. Black Tern
10. Black Duck
11. Canada Goose
12. Pintail
13. Pied-billed Grebe
14. Florida Gallinule

## SKY SILHOUETTES

1. Barn Swallow
2. Purple Martin
3. Chimney Swift
4. House Sparrow
5. Starling
6. Grackle
7. Robin
8. Flicker
9. Mourning Dove
10. Kingfisher
11. Crow
12. Sharp-shinned Hawk
13. Sparrow Hawk
14. Meadowlark

# INDEX

Only English names are given. Page numbers in italic figures indicate main descriptions accompanied by illustrations. Other references are often merely a brief mention of the species.